Animation for Kids
with Scratch Programming

Create Your Own Digital Art, Games, and Stories with Code

Dedicated to my little sister, Abbey Takeuchi for her artistic talent and boundless imagination.

by Danny Takeuchi

MentorsCloud

Boise, Idaho

Animation for Kids with Scratch Programming. Copyright © 2015 Danny Takeuchi

Library of Congress Control Number: 2015915069
Published in Boise, Idaho
By MentorsCloud

ISBN-10: 978-0692527573
ISBN-13: 0692527575

Available from Amazon.com, MentorsCloud.com, and other retail outlets.

For information on distribution, translation, or bulk sales, please contact MentorsCloud directly:
info@mentorscloud.com; www.MentorsCloud.com

Table of Contents

Section 1: Programming Fundamentals

Section 2: Animation Techniques

Section 3: Super Duper Animations

Introduction

What is Scratch?

Scratch is a visual programming language developed by the Massachusetts Institute of Technology (MIT) Media Lab's Lifelong Kindergarten Group. This software is a great learning platform for students from 8 years old and up to learn how to code. You can use drag and drop command blocks in Scratch to create sensational animations and games. By learning how to code, you are joining a global coding community of young dreamers, doers, and creators.

Before You Start:

- Download Scratch 2.0 from *https://scratch.mit.edu/scratch2download/* Scratch can run on Mac, Windows, and Linux. Follow the appropriate set of instructions on MIT's website for your operating system.
- Download a Snapshot or Snipping Tool to your computer.
    - Windows: **Snipping Tool**. This tool comes with Windows.
    - OS X: **Snip**. Download this tool from Apple's App Store.
- Download our online resources for this book by going to www.MentorsCloud.com. Use the user name mc2319 and enter your email and password to register. If you want approved access within 24 hours, please send us an email at info@MentorsCloud.com. Check your junk folder in case our confirmation email lands there.
- You will need our online resources to import sprites, backdrops, and sound files for your projects. Please download both *Resources.zip* and *FinishedProjects.zip* to your Scratch folder. Use the templates, sprites, and sound files from *Resources.zip* when instructed to build your projects. *FinishedProjects.zip* contains the completed animations and provides a reference point for budding programmers.
- Create a folder for your own Scratch projects. By storing all of your animations in one place, your files will be organized and easy to find.

Whom This Book is for:

This book is an introduction to computer programming for students 8 years and up. It can be used as a classroom textbook or as a self-study guide. This book is dedicated to kids who love art and creativity regardless of whether they are math or science inclined.

How This Book is organized:

This book has three sections:

- Section one starts with simple projects to help students learn basic programming concepts. Those projects give students the hands-on learning experience needed to develope their own games and animations.
- Section two provides students with animation techniques to fuel their creativity and imagination. It provides them tools to create more interesting animations.
- Section three guides students through four complete animations, each with its own storyboard. Kids learn how to manage the complexities of development, the interactions of multiple characters, and the timing of separate events. Many of the animation techniques introduced earlier are utilized to create these projects.

Free webinar classes included with the book purchase:

Two hours of free webinar classes are included with the purchase of this book. In this online class, we will walk students through the first chapter. To register for the free webinar, please go to www.MentorsCloud.com.

Credits:

Ch. 15 Snapshot Technique: *Aquarium 2hr relax music*, by milleaccendini
Ch. 16 Oil in the Ocean Documentary: *Ophelia's Song* by Grapes
These recordings are licensed under
https://creativecommons.org/licenses/by/4.0/legalcode.

About the Author:

Danny Takeuchi is the founder of the startup, MentorsCloud.com. He taught over 200 kids how to program games, animations, and mobile apps, using his own curriculum. He is also a collaborator in the Sherlock Holmes & the Internet of Things (IoT) Global Challenge sponsored by Columbia University's Digital Storytelling Lab. He worked as an engineering intern in the HP Inc. R&D Lab. For more information, go to www.MentorsCloud.com.

Chapter 1 - Learning the Basics

The Animation:

The Cat dances to the beat. It then sneaks up behind the Bat and kicks him off the screen.

What You Will Learn:

- Basic Movement and Speech
- Graphic Effects and Sound
- Block Repetition
- Broadcast

1. Start Moving

Open a new Scratch project, and go to the **Motion** section. Drag a **Move Steps** block into the scripts area. Notice that all the motion blocks are blue.

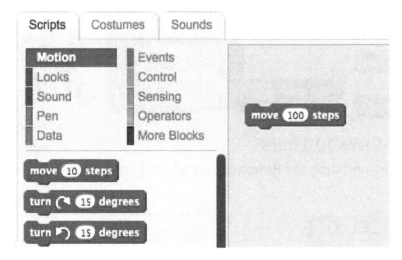

Click the number inside the block, and change it to 100. To move the cat, click the block. When the cat moves 100 steps, it's actually moving 100 pixels, which is roughly one inch.

 Move the cat to the center of the screen with the **Go To** block. Otherwise, it would start where it left off in the previous program. At the center, the x and y positions equal 0.

Now click these blocks. Oops! The cat is moving too fast for us to see! That's fine. Keep your eyes open, and we will address this later.

2. Add a Drum Beat

Go to the **Sound** section. Click and drag the **Play Drum** block onto your screen.

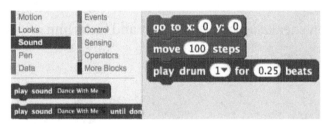

The more beats, the longer the sound.

Click your blocks and listen.

3. Move Back and Forth to the Beat

Change the first **Move Steps** block to 20 steps. Then, add another **Move Steps** block, and enter -20 steps. The minus sign moves the cat left instead of right. Add another **Play Drum** block, and choose **Crash Cymbal (4)** by clicking the dropdown menu. Don't forget to click, and see what happens!

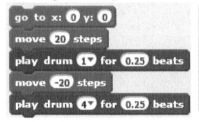
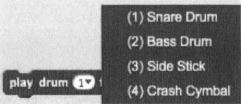

4. Repeat Dance Moves 10 Times

Click the **Control** section, and drag the **Repeat** block around every block except the **Go To** block.

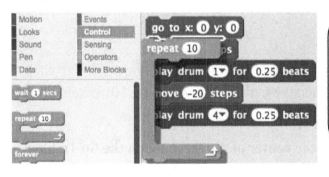

-The **Repeat** block runs the dance steps inside 10 times.
-Use the **Forever** block if you want to keep on repeating.

2

5. Start Talking

Click the **Looks** section, and drag a **Say For 1 Secs** block above the **Repeat** block. Below, drag a **Say For 1 Secs** block and a **Think for 2 Secs** block. Insert the below phrases into each block.

Dance with me!

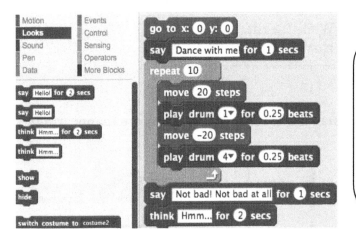

Make sure you drag the **Say** and **Think** blocks that end with **For _ Secs**. Without specifying the time, each message will stay on the screen forever.

6. Attach the Start Switch

Click the **Events** section, and drag a **Key Pressed** block and a **Green Flag** block into your scripts. **Events** blocks decide when to run your scripts.

To begin the program, click the **Green Flag**.

To stop the program, click the **Red Stop Sign**.

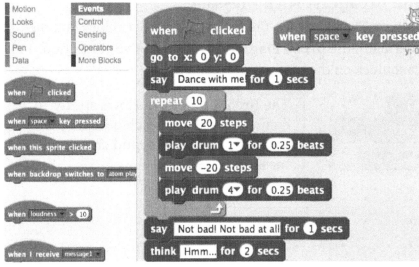

7. Add Graphic Effects

Click the **Looks** section, and drag the blocks below:

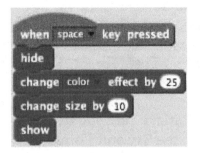

The **Hide/Show** blocks make the cat disappear and reappear.

While the cat is hiding, it changes color and grows.

But what if we want the cat to stay hidden for some time before reappearing? Again the cat is too fast.

But wait! Let's not forget the **Wait** block from the **Control** section. Insert this into your script, and see what happens.

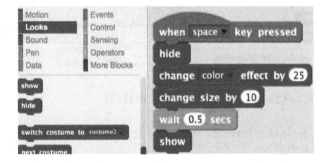

Notice how the cat remains hidden for a half-second before re-appearing due to the **Wait** block. Experiment with different graphic effects by clicking the dropdown menu. Have fun!

8. Reset Cat and Broadcast Kick Message

Click the **Looks** section. Then, drag the **Clear Graphic Effects** block and the **Set Size** block underneath the **Green Flag** block. Go to the **Events** section, and place the **Broadcast** block on the bottom.

The **Broadcast** block allows sprites to communicate with each other. Open the dropdown menu, and create a new message, "**Kick**".

4

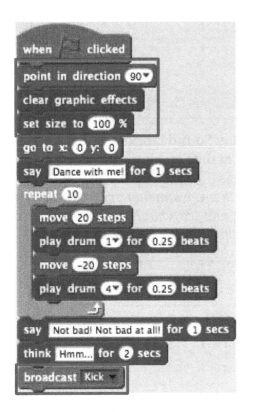

The cat's size, graphic effects, and direction carry into the next program. Therefore, we must reset the **Cat** sprite back to normal at the beginning of this program.

9. Add Sound

Click the **Sounds** tab Scripts Costumes Sounds . You can choose a sound from the Scratch Sound library, record your own, or import a sound file from your computer. For now, let's add the sound, **Laugh-Male,** from the sound library.

Next, record your own sound, "**Dance With Me**". New sound: Dance With Me

Click the ● to record your voice. You can edit the sound, and delete parts of it by using Edit ▼ Effects ▼ .

Click the **Scripts** tab, and drag play sound Dance with me ▼ from the **Sound** section. Make sure the right song is selected from the drop down menu.

Here is the Cat's Dance Script with sound added.

The **Play Sound** block is placed ahead of the **Say** block. What happens if you switch the order? **Note:** *In programming, try different things, and see what happens. This will help you perfect your program.*

10. Program the Cat's Kick

Drag the blocks on the right into your script. The **Turn** blocks are in the **Motion** section.

Provides more fluid motion compared to the **Go To** and **Move Steps** blocks.

Both **Repeat** blocks split the cat's single rotation into multiple rotations with **Wait** blocks. This slows down the speedy cat so we can see him drawing his foot back and launching it forward.

11. Add the Bat Sprite and Rename your Cat

Bat1

Sprites are objects that are programmed with specific actions. The cat is every project's starter sprite. Click 🌱 from the sprite pane to add another sprite from the Scratch Sprite Library. Choose **Bat1**.

Let's change our **Sprite1**'s name. Click 🛈 and type "Cat".

12. Program the Bat's Flight

Click **Bat1** from your sprite panel. Each sprite has it's own script and blocks. *Make sure you don't accidentally drag the bat's blocks into the cat's script.* First, let's give the bat its starting properties.

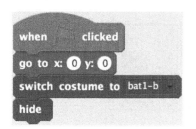

Hide in the center of the screen with wings folded until it receives the **Kick** broadcast.

Go to the **Events** section, and drag two **When I Receive Kick** blocks onto your script. You can find the **Next Costume** block in the **Looks** section and the **Forever** and **If** blocks in the **Control** section.

Go to the **Sensing** section to find the **Touching** block. Hover the left corner of this block above the space inside the **If** block. Drop it inside.

Now let's program the bat to fly off the screen while flapping its wings.

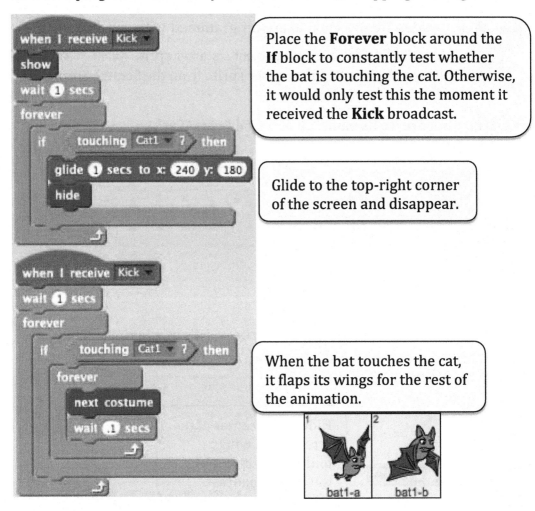

Place the **Forever** block around the **If** block to constantly test whether the bat is touching the cat. Otherwise, it would only test this the moment it received the **Kick** broadcast.

Glide to the top-right corner of the screen and disappear.

When the bat touches the cat, it flaps its wings for the rest of the animation.

13. Save your Project

Go to the **File** tab on the top of the screen. Click **Save**, and name your project. The next time you **Save**, this animation will save under its current name.

If you want to save your project under a different name, choose **Save as**. You can also start a blank project by clicking **New,** or you open a saved project by clicking **Open**.

Click the **Green Flag,** and watch your first animation!

8

Chapter 2 - Disco Pop

The Animation:

Disco Pop alternates between three stage settings with flashing neon lights and music. The Cat, Ballerina, and Break-dancer dance on the stage.

What You Will Learn:

- Animated Sprites and Stage
- Time Intervals
- Paint the Backdrop

1. Add the Ballerina and Breakdancer1 Sprites

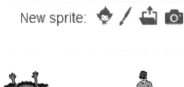

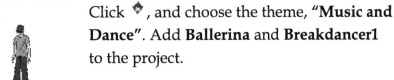

Click ❀, and choose the theme, **"Music and Dance"**. Add **Ballerina** and **Breakdancer1** to the project.

2. Draw Lights on the Stage Backdrop

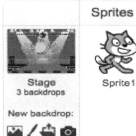

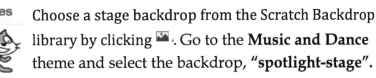

Choose a stage backdrop from the Scratch Backdrop library by clicking ▣. Go to the **Music and Dance** theme and select the backdrop, **"spotlight-stage"**.

Click on the **Stage,** and go to the **Backdrops** tab. Right-click the white backdrop and delete it. Or, click the x on the top right hand corner of the selected backdrop.

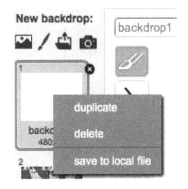

9

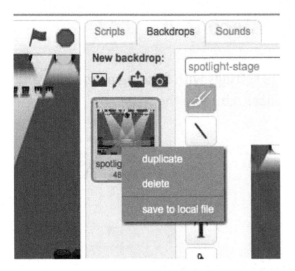

Right-click **spotlight-stage** and duplicate it. Do this twice so you have three identical backdrops.

Let's give the stage some lights. Click the second backdrop, and draw circles ONLY on the wall. Then, click the third backdrop and draw rectangles ONLY on the wall.

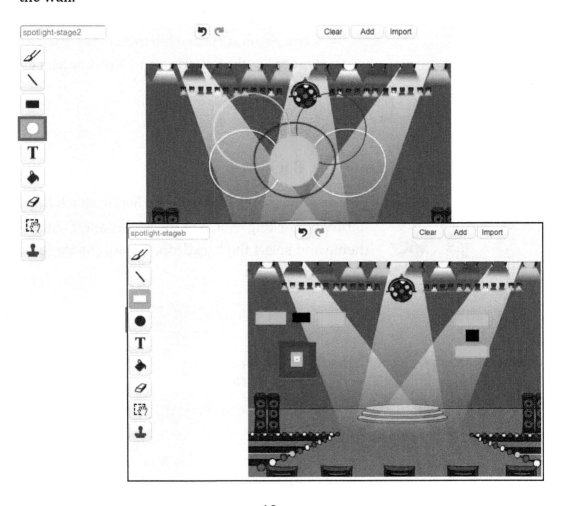

3. Add Stage Lights and Music

Click the **Script** tab. Make sure the **Stage** is selected so that you don't program the wrong object. Drag the **Switch Backdrop and Wait** blocks from the **Looks** section, and drag the **Forever** and **Wait** blocks from the **Control** section onto the screen.

The **Wait** blocks prevent your lights from flashing too quickly.

Click the **Green Flag** and see what happens.

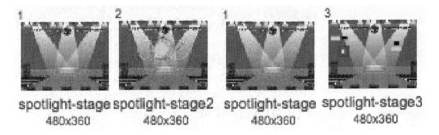

spotlight-stage spotlight-stage2   spotlight-stage   spotlight-stage3
480x360   480x360   480x360   480x360

Now, let's add background music. Go to the **Sound** tab, and click 🔊 to add "Hip Hop". Navigate to the **Sound** section, and drag the **Play Sound Until Done** block onto the script. Then, replay **Hip Hop** over and over with the **Forever** block.

hip hop

4. Make the Ballerina Dance

Click the **Ballerina** sprite, and go to the **Scripts** tab. Drag the blocks in the figure below onto the screen.

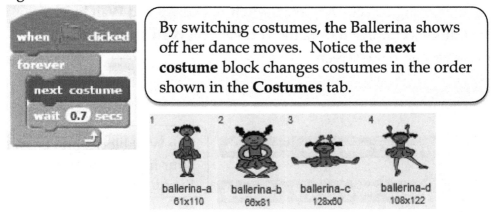

By switching costumes, the Ballerina shows off her dance moves. Notice the **next costume** block changes costumes in the order shown in the **Costumes** tab.

ballerina-a 61x110   ballerina-b 66x81   ballerina-c 128x60   ballerina-d 108x122

5. Have Ballerina Dance Across the Stage

So far, the ballerina only dances in the same place. Let's have her hop across the stage by dragging the blocks below. You can find the **Set Rotation Style Block** in the **Motion** section.

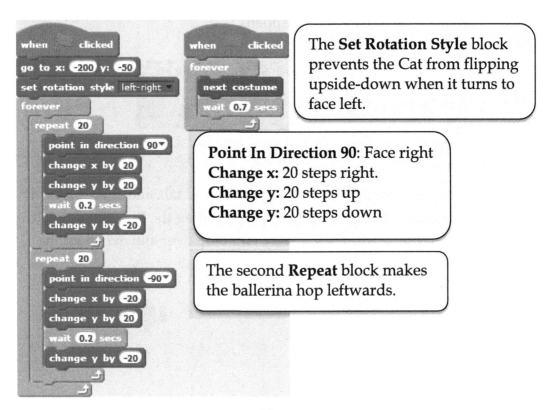

The **Set Rotation Style** block prevents the Cat from flipping upside-down when it turns to face left.

Point In Direction 90: Face right
Change x: 20 steps right.
Change y: 20 steps up
Change y: 20 steps down

The second **Repeat** block makes the ballerina hop leftwards.

6. Have Cat Glide Across the Stage

Click the **Cat** sprite, and make him slide back and forth.

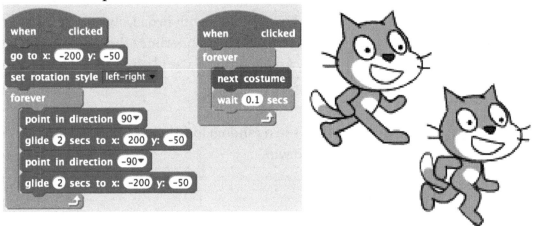

7. Program Break-dancer's Dance Moves

Now let's go to the **Breakdancer1** sprite and show his dance moves.

Places the **Breakdancer1** sprite on the stage platform.

breakdancer1-a   breakdancer1-b   breakdancer1-c

Click the **Green Flag,** and watch the party!

Chapter 3 - Catch the Cat

The Animation:

The Cat traces "HI" in a rainbow of colors with broad, sweeping movements and short, jerky movements. Next, it underlines the message, "HI", while ghosting and changing color. And finally, the Cat plays hide and seek.

The Game:

The Cat hides and reappears in a random location every 2 seconds. Catch the Cat at least three times to win.

What You Will Learn:

- Pen Blocks
- Variables
- Random Operator
- Fix Programming Bugs

1. Set the Cat's Starting Position

Start at the upper-left hand corner of the screen.

2. Draw the H

Use the **Glide** block to move the cat in an H.

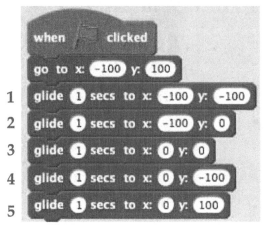

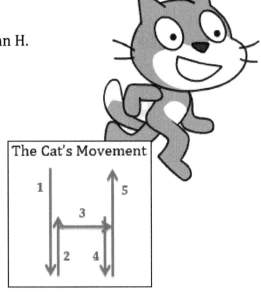

3. Draw the I

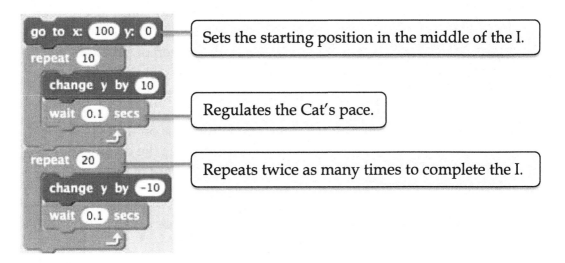

go to x: 100 y: 0 — Sets the starting position in the middle of the I.

wait 0.1 secs — Regulates the Cat's pace.

repeat 20 — Repeats twice as many times to complete the I.

4. Combine the H and I Scripts into HI

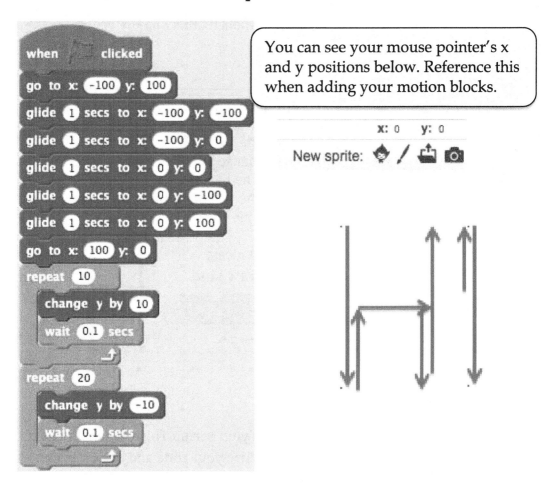

You can see your mouse pointer's x and y positions below. Reference this when adding your motion blocks.

x: 0   y: 0

New sprite:

5. Trace "HI" with Color

```
when        clicked
go to x: -100  y: 100
show
clear graphic effects
1  clear
2  set pen size to 10
3  pen down
glide 1 secs to x: -100  y: -100
glide 1 secs to x: -100  y: 0
```

Click the **Pen** section, and insert three green blocks into the code.
1. Clear the screen of previous pen marks.
2. Make the pen larger and more visible.
3. Trace the color on the background as the cat moves.

Click the **Green Flag** to test your program.

Uh Oh! It looks like we ran into a bug! No, it's not an insect. It's a programming bug, or an error in our programming logic.

When crossing over from the H to the I, the cat kept on tracing. This makes the I look like a funky Y. Lets fix this bug by inserting the blocks below.

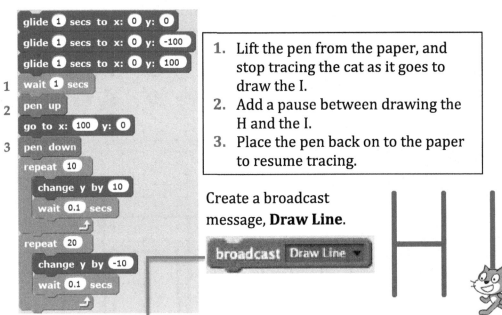

```
glide 1 secs to x: 0 y: 0
glide 1 secs to x: 0 y: -100
glide 1 secs to x: 0 y: 100
1  wait 1 secs
2  pen up
   go to x: 100  y: 0
3  pen down
   repeat 10
      change y by 10
      wait 0.1 secs
   repeat 20
      change y by -10
      wait 0.1 secs
```

1. Lift the pen from the paper, and stop tracing the cat as it goes to draw the I.
2. Add a pause between drawing the H and the I.
3. Place the pen back on to the paper to resume tracing.

Create a broadcast message, **Draw Line**.

```
broadcast Draw Line ▼
```

Place this **broadcast** block on the bottom of your script. This triggers the next part of the program. **Broadcast** blocks organize your code and keep it from getting too big.

6. Trace with a Rainbow of Colors

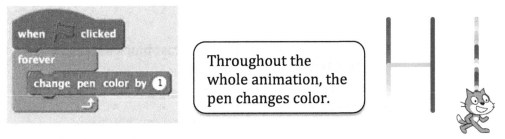

Throughout the whole animation, the pen changes color.

7. Underline Hi

Next, the cat will trace a line underneath the message, "HI". When **Draw Line** is broadcasted, change the line's size, color effects, ghost effects, and add some sound.

```
when I receive  Draw Line ▼
set pen size to 5
change color ▼ effect by 20
change ghost ▼ effect by 10
play drum 15▼ for 0.25 beats
```

Now let's program the cat's motion.

```
set rotation style  left-right ▼
pen up
glide 1 secs to x: -180 y: -135
pen down
point in direction 90▼
glide 1 secs to x: 180 y: -135
point in direction -90▼
```

Combine both sets of blocks, and place a **Repeat 10** block around them. This makes the Cat underline "HI" 10 times, each time in a different color.

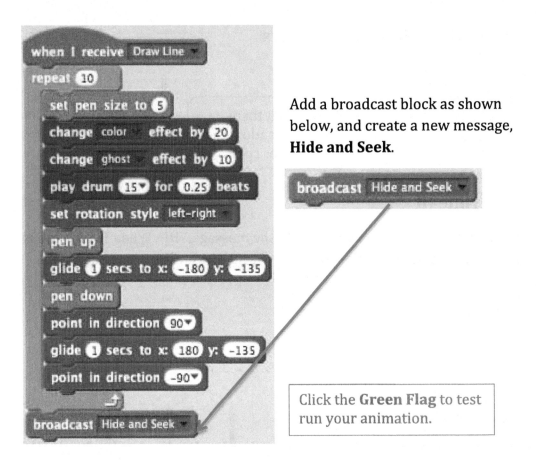

Add a broadcast block as shown below, and create a new message, **Hide and Seek**.

Click the **Green Flag** to test run your animation.

8. Create the Score Variable

Variables keep track of certain value changes such as the score. Create a **Score** variable to monitor the number of times the cat is clicked.

First, click the **Data** section. Choose the **Make a Variable** button 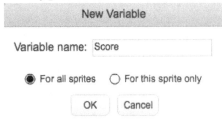, and type **Score**.

New Variable
Variable name: Score
⦿ For all sprites ○ For this sprite only
OK   Cancel

Select **For all sprites** if you want to use **Score** for multiple sprites. If you want each sprite to have its own **Score**, then choose **For this sprite only**.
After you create this variable, a new collection of blocks should appear in the **Data** section.

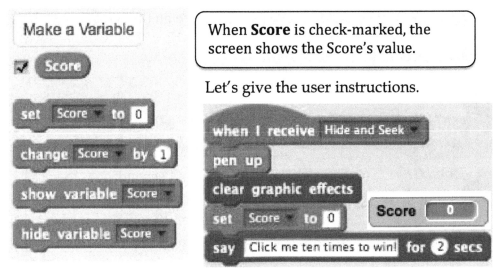

When **Score** is check-marked, the screen shows the Score's value.

Let's give the user instructions.

Click the **Green Flag** to test your program. Whoops! The cat might not have reappeared on the screen. Like before, the properties of the previous program carried over. We must make it reappear at the start of the project.

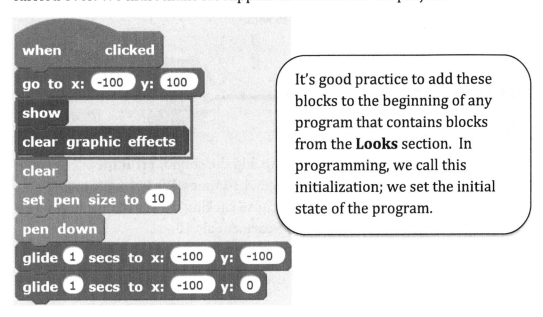

It's good practice to add these blocks to the beginning of any program that contains blocks from the **Looks** section. In programming, we call this initialization; we set the initial state of the program.

9. Program the Game

Drag a **Go To** block to your scripts, and go to the **Operators** section. Drag two **Pick Random blocks,** and enter their values as **-200 to 200** and **-160 to 160**.

Place the **Pick Random** blocks into the x and y positions of the **Go To** block by hovering the left edge of the **Operator** blocks over each oval-shaped space.

The **Go To** block now moves the cat to a random place on the screen. Next, let's make the cat disappear and reappear.

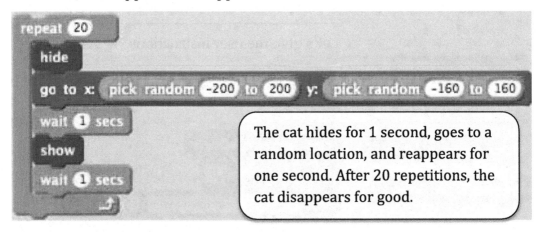

The cat hides for 1 second, goes to a random location, and reappears for one second. After 20 repetitions, the cat disappears for good.

Let's program a way to catch the cat when it appears. Go to the **Events** section and find the **When this Sprite Clicked** block.

Next, go to the **Sound** Tab, and click ◀€ to add the sound, **Triumph**.

The user wins when the cat has been clicked 10 times. We just have to test how many times the cat has been clicked. Because clicking the cat changes **Score** by 1, we need to end the animation when **Score** equals 10.

Retrieve an **If** block, and place ◁▷ inside it from the **Operators** section. Place (Score) into the first white space, and type 9 in the second white space.

Insert the blocks boxed in red. After the cat is clicked 10 times, it plays the sound, **Triumph**, congratulates the user, and hides. If not, the cat says, "Game Over!"

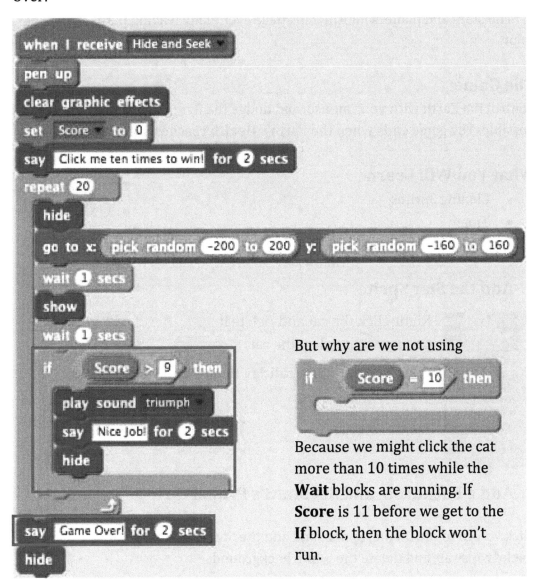

But why are we not using

Because we might click the cat more than 10 times while the **Wait** blocks are running. If **Score** is 11 before we get to the **If** block, then the block won't run.

Click the **Green Flag,** and enjoy your animation!

Chapter 4 - Star Storm

The Animation:

The stars and planets multiply in space eventually leaving paths of blazing color.

The Game:

Control the Earth with your mouse, and dodge the flying stars for as long as possible. The game ends when the Earth's **Health** reaches 0.

What You Will Learn:

- Cloning Sprites
- Timer
- Stamp

1. Add the Star Sprite

Right-click the cat and delete it.
Or, use ✄ to delete the cat.

Click 🐱, go to the **Holiday** theme, and choose **Star3**.

2. Add a Backdrop, and Set Star3's Properties

Click 🖼, go to the theme, **Space**, and add the **Stars** backdrop. Then, go to the **Backdrops** tab, and delete the white background.

Now let's set the star's starting characteristics.

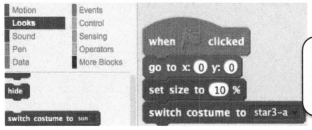

Goes to the center, decreases the size, and switches to the appropriate costume.

3. Create Clones of Stars

Clones allow you to duplicate **Star3** without having to create and program lots of other star sprites. This saves you both space and time. Clones can be used to simulate rain, falling cats, blazing fireballs, etc. The possibilities are endless!

Click the **Control** section, and add the three blocks boxed in red.

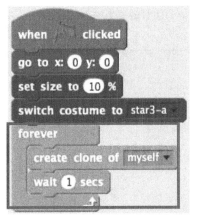

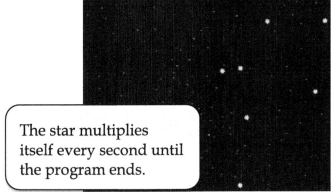

The star multiplies itself every second until the program ends.

4. Program Each Clone to Move and Bounce

Each clone does the SAME THING... with one exception, the **Random** operator.

Click the **Control** section, and start your script with the **When I Start as a Clone** block.

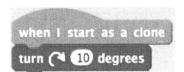

Turns the star clones so that they fly diagonally across the screen.

Click the **Operators** section, and insert a **Pick Random** block into the **Turn** block.

Enter 100 and 300 into the **Pick Random** block.

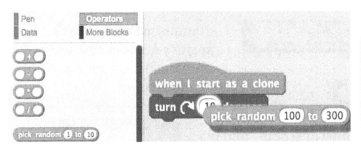

Each star clone turns anywhere between 100 and 300 degrees to add some variation.

Now let's make each star clone move in the direction its facing. When it reaches the edge, it will bounce.

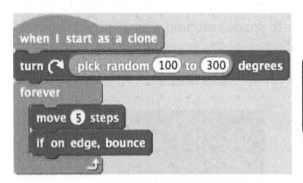

Star clones move towards the direction they turned to and bounce off the edge off the screen.

5. Add Costumes to the Star Sprite

Click the **Costumes** tab, and delete the costume, **star3-b.**

Underneath the **Costumes** tab, click  to upload other sprites. These sprites will be **Star3's** costumes.

Add the three costumes below:

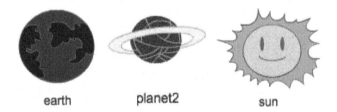

earth   planet2   sun

6. Create Flashy Trails of Stars and Planets

To imprint images of **Star3** on the backdrop, drag the **Stamp** block from the **Pen** section.

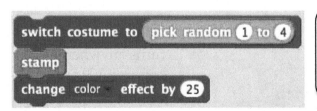

Stamps one of the **Star3** sprite's random costumes onto the background and changes color.

Drag the **If** block from the **Control** section, and place inside it a **>** block from the **Operators** section.

Interpreting OPERATOR blocks:

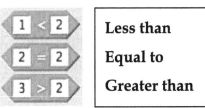

1 < 2	Less than
2 = 2	Equal to
3 > 2	Greater than

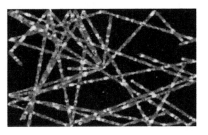

Let's start stamping **Star3** on the background after 5 seconds. Click the **Sensing** section, and find the oval-shaped **Timer** block 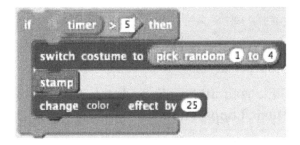. This block represents the number of seconds that passed since the start of the program.

When the **timer** reaches 5 seconds, the blocks inside the **If...then** block run. Otherwise, they are skipped.

Place the **If** block inside the **Forever** block at the bottom.

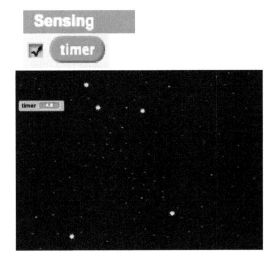

25

7. Fix the Bug

When you try to restart the program, the color won't go away! Click the **Pen** section, and add the **Clear** block. This block removes the stamps from the screen.

8. Add Background Music

Go to your **Stage's Sound**s tab, and click . Find the theme, **Music Loops**, and choose the sound, **Techno**.

Now go back to your **Scripts** tab, and play this sound during the animation.

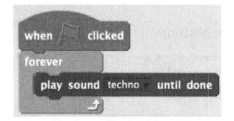

techno

9. Save Your Progress and Test the Animation

Go to **File > Save As.** Save your project under the name, "**Twinkle Twinkle Little Star**". Click the **Green Flag** to test this animation.

Now let's change this animation into a game. Save the "**Twinkle Twinkle Little Star**" animation as "**Star Storm**". This reuses the code for the new project. We just have to make slight adjustments.

10.   Remove the Pen Aspect from Star Clones

Go to the **Star3** sprite, and remove several blocks.

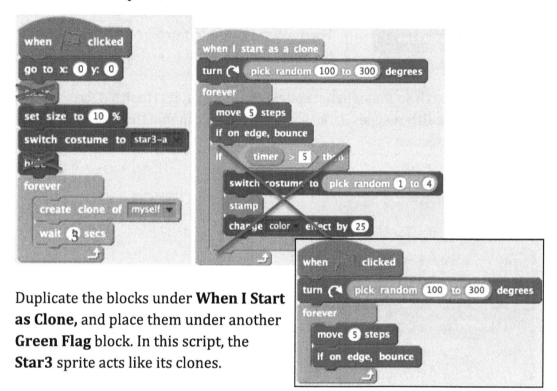

Duplicate the blocks under **When I Start as Clone,** and place them under another **Green Flag** block. In this script, the **Star3** sprite acts like its clones.

11.   Add Earth Sprite

Click ☁, go to the **Space** theme, and add **Earth**.

Go to the **Data** section, and create the variable, **Health, for all sprites**. In the game, the **Health** of the **Earth** starts at 100. Let's first give the sprite its starting properties.

Earth

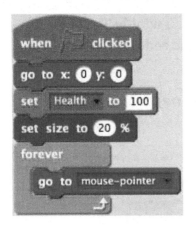

Makes **Earth** the same size as **Star3**.

The mouse pointer controls the earth's movement.

Program the **Earth** so that when it collides with a star, its **Health** decreases by 10. When its **Health** reaches 0, the game ends. You can find the **Stop All** block in the **Control** section.

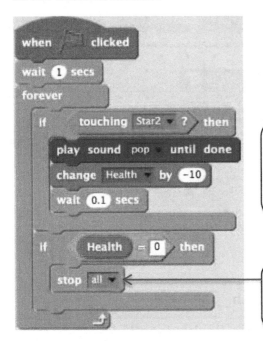

The **Earth** takes 10 points of damage when it collides with **Star3**. It then takes a split-second until the Earth can be hit again.

This block stops the whole program like the **Red Stop Sign.**

Click the **Green Flag** to test your game. Remember to save the changes to your **Star Storm** project.

Chapter 5 - Birthday Cake Lift

The Animation:

Lift the Cake towards Gobo for his birthday, and release 50 balloons into the air.

What You Will Learn:

- Video Motion
- Broadcast
- Sensing

1. Add Gobo, Cake, and Balloon Sprites from the Library

Right click the **Cat** sprite and delete it. We won't be using it.

Gobo Cake Balloon1

Click ◇. Go to the **Fantasy** category for **Gobo**. Then go to the **Things** category for **Cake** and **Balloon1**.

2. Set up the Instructions

Let's program **Gobo** to give the user instructions. Underneath, broadcast a new message, **start**.

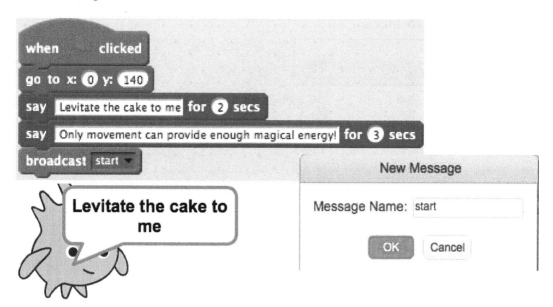

3. Prepare the Cake

Click the **Cake** sprite, and set its starting properties. Go to the **Sensing** section for the **Turn Video On** block.

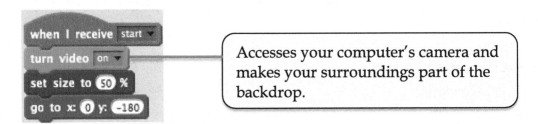

Accesses your computer's camera and makes your surroundings part of the backdrop.

4. Simulate the Cake's Gravity

The Cake slowly drops to the ground throughout the animation.

Only movement can provide enough magical energy!

We need to measure the amount of movement registered by the **Video** block to lift the cake.

Go to the **Sensing** section, and find `video motion on this sprite`. Place this block inside a **>** block.

Insert 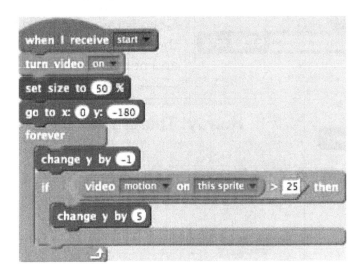 inside the **If** block, and put everything together.

5. Test if Cake Reaches Gobo

Click the **Gobo** sprite. We need to constantly test when the cake reaches Gobo to trigger the end of the animation.

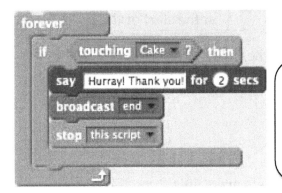

The Gobo continues to touch cake after it has been touched for the first time. The **Stop** block prevents **Forever** from broadcasting **end** multiple times.

Place these blocks under the instructional blocks of **Step 2**.

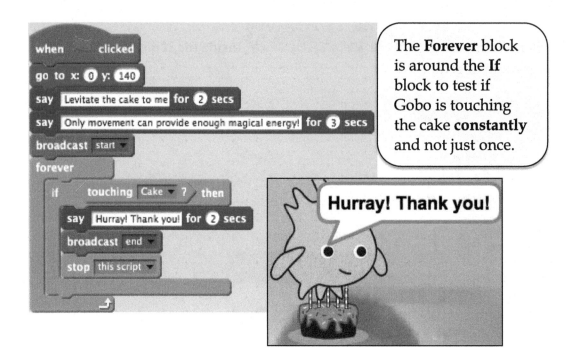

6. Release the Balloons

Go to **Balloon3's Sound** tab, and click to add the sound, **birthday**.

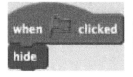

birthday

> Keeps the balloon hidden at the start of the program.

Play, **birthday**, when Gobo is touching the Cake.

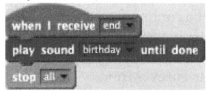

One balloon is not adequate for a party. Lets make 50!

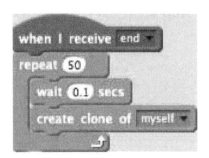

> Multiplies the balloon 50 times at .1-second intervals.

Program each balloon clone to float towards the ceiling.

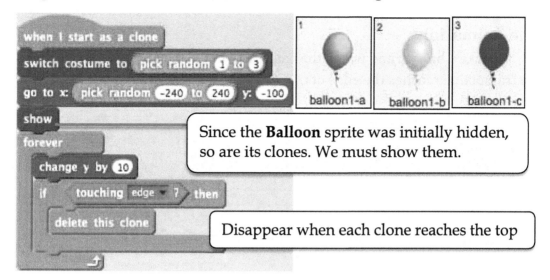

Since the **Balloon** sprite was initially hidden, so are its clones. We must show them.

Disappear when each clone reaches the top

Click the **Green Flag,** and watch your first animation!

Chapter 6 - Basketball Toss

The Animation:

Make a basket, and watch the basketball bounce on a trampoline until the trampoline reaches the edge of the stage.

What You Will Learn:

- Simulate Free Fall
- Color Sensing
- Variables

1. Add a Basketball Sprite from the Library.

Right click the **Cat** sprite, and delete it.

Click ◈ to add new sprites. Choose the **Sports** theme for the **Basketball** sprite, and the **Things** category for the **Trampoline** sprite.

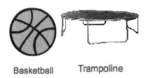

Basketball   Trampoline

2. Add a Basketball Court Backdrop

Click 🖼 to add a different backdrop. Go to the **Sports** theme, and choose **basketball-court1-b**.

basketball-court1-b

Next, click the **Stage,** and go to the **Backdrops** tab to remove the other white background.

Select the **basketball-court1-b** backdrop. We need to move the basket in this picture to the right side. Switch the left and right sides of the backdrop by going to the top right-hand corner of the your paint editor and clicking ▣.

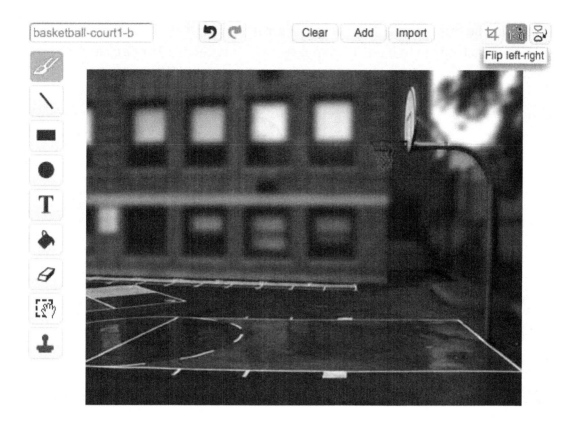

3. Set the Basketball's Properties

Click the **Basketball** sprite, and give it several starting features.

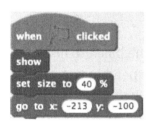

Decreases the basketball's size to fit the hoops and starts it at the free throw line.

Now let's create an **x speed** and **y speed** variable in order to keep track of the basketball's up-down and left-right speed. Click the **Data** section. Choose Make a Variable , and type the variable name **"x speed"**.

If you choose this variable **For all sprites**, then multiple sprites will use it. If you want each sprite to have its own **x speed**, then choose **For this sprite only**.

Basketball

Use the same process to create a "**y speed**" variable.
Once you created a variable, **Data** blocks will appear in the menu.

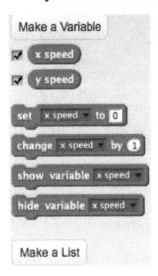

Drag two **Set** blocks into the script. Remember, **x speed** is the basketball sprite's speed in the left/right directions and **y speed** is its speed in the up/down directions.

Let's program the basketball's midair trajectory. You can find the **Touching Color** block inside the **Sensing** section.

36

Set the color for the **Sensing** block by clicking inside touching color ■ ? and then clicking the basketball hoop's red rim. When the basketball hits the rim, it will change its motion.

4. Put your Blocks Together

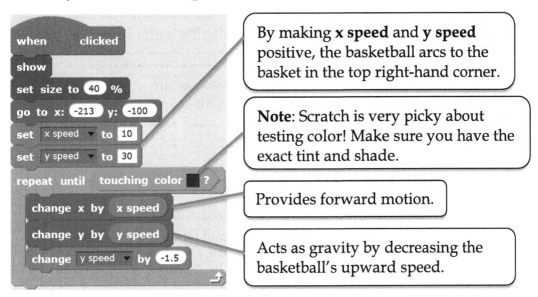

By making **x speed** and **y speed** positive, the basketball arcs to the basket in the top right-hand corner.

Note: Scratch is very picky about testing color! Make sure you have the exact tint and shade.

Provides forward motion.

Acts as gravity by decreasing the basketball's upward speed.

5. Simulate the First Bounce

Go to the **Sensing** section, and drag two **Touching Color** blocks into the script. Both are pre-assigned a random color. Reset these colors to the blackish-blue of the pavement and the greyish-white of the building.

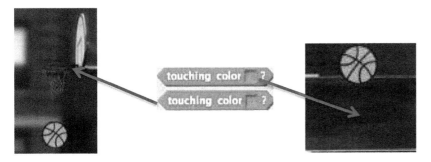

Let's program the first bounce. You can find the **Wait Until** block in the **Control** section.

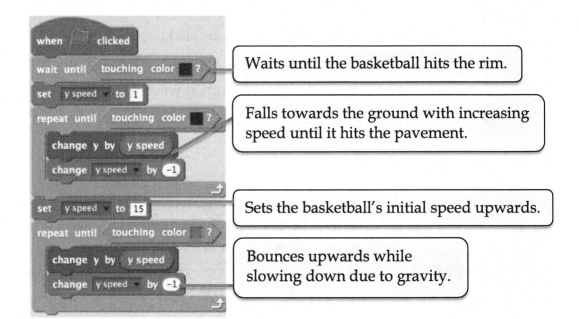

Waits until the basketball hits the rim.

Falls towards the ground with increasing speed until it hits the pavement.

Sets the basketball's initial speed upwards.

Bounces upwards while slowing down due to gravity.

6. Simulate the Second Bounce

Duplicate everything but the top two blocks by right-clicking the **Set y speed to 1** block. The blocks used to program the second bounce are incredibly similar to those of the first bounce. We just have to adjust the color and **y speed**.

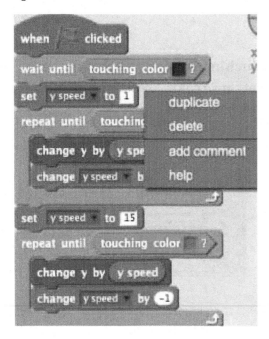

Set **y speed** to 0 instead of 1. Delete the second half of the duplicated blocks, create a trampoline broadcast, and put 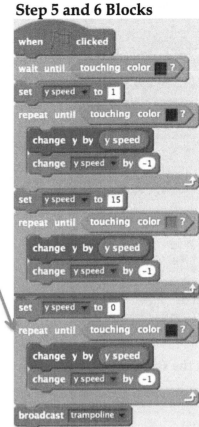 at the bottom.

Step 5 and 6 Blocks

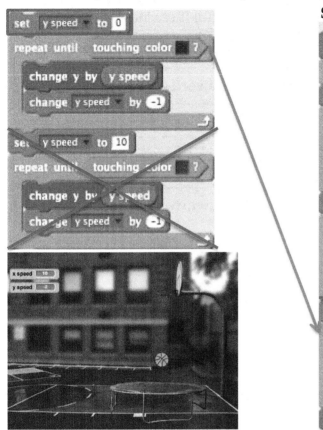

7. Program the Trampoline Sprite

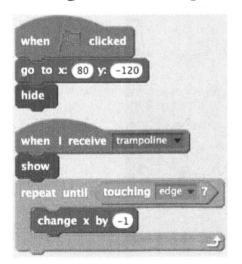

Hides under the basketball hoop at the start of the program

Appears and inches towards the left side of the screen until touching the edge.

39

8. Bounce the Basketball on the Trampoline

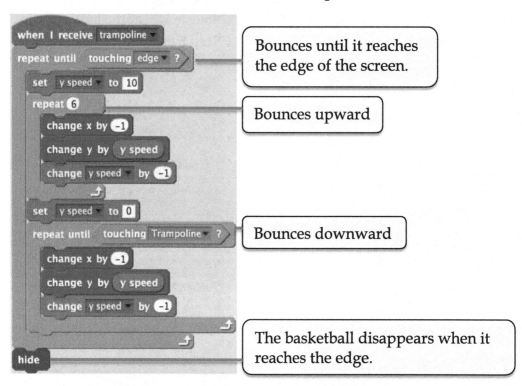

```
when I receive trampoline ▾
repeat until   touching edge ▾ ?
    set  y speed ▾ to 10
    repeat 6
        change x by -1
        change y by  y speed
        change y speed ▾ by -1
    set  y speed ▾ to 0
    repeat until   touching Trampoline ▾ ?
        change x by -1
        change y by  y speed
        change y speed ▾ by -1
hide
```

Bounces until it reaches the edge of the screen.

Bounces upward

Bounces downward

The basketball disappears when it reaches the edge.

Click the **Green Flag,** and enjoy your animation!

Chapter 7 - Rescue Mission

The Animation:

The Witch kidnaps the Princess, and the Prince embarks on a mission to rescue her. He must survive the Bat of the Dark Forest and defeat the Witch's pet Dragon.

The Game:

The Prince shoots Lightening Bolts at the Dragon while avoiding its Fireballs. If the Dragon is shot 5 times, it dies and the Prince rescues the Princess.

What You Will Learn:

- Creating a Storyboard
- Managing Multiple Sprites' Interaction

1. Create the Storyboard

Right click the cat sprite, and delete it. Click 🐾 to add the other sprites:

| Witch | Prince | Princess | Dragon | Bat2 | Lightning | Beachball |

Rename the **Beachball** sprite, **Fireball**. To keep your screen neat while programming this bigger project, hide every sprite for now.

Now lets create a storyline to help guide this project. The words in quotes will be written on each scene's backdrop.

Scene 1 - Bedroom: *"Once upon a time, there was a princess, the fairest in the land."*
Princess: *What a fine morning!*
Witch: *Come with me, my pretty!*
Princess: *aeieiehh!*
Scene 2 – Enter Prince : *"When the Prince heard of her distress, he rushed to her aid."*
Prince: *Don't worry! I will come to the rescue!*
Scene 3 – Dark Forest: *"The Prince plunged into the dark forest."*
(Bat flies at Prince)
Prince: *Hiyah!*

Scene 4 – Fight the Dragon: *"And he fought the Witch's pet Dragon."*
(Prince shoots the Lighting bolts and avoids the Fireballs to defeat Dragon)
Witch: *NOOOOO!*
Scene 5 – The End: *"The Prince rescued the Princess and they lived happily ever after."*
Princess: *My hero!*

Delete the white background, and click 🖼 to add your backdrops in this order:

2. Type the Storyline onto your Backdrops

Click the **Text** button. Type the words for **Scene 1 – Bedroom1**. Press the enter key to start a new line when you run out of space.

bedroom1

Type the quoted storylines in the other backdrops as shown below.

But before typing the storyline for **castle3**, switch the left and right sides of the picture by clicking ⟳ on the top right-hand corner.

castle1   **castle3**

woods   **sparkling**

Let's go to the **Stage**'s **Script** tab, and lay out each scene. This is the **Storyboard Script**.

Create a new broadcast message for each scene in our **Storyboard Script** to create a clear sequence of events. This prevents confusion when working with multiple sprites. **The End** scene is an exception.

Caution: Make sure the broadcast blocks end with **and wait,** or every scene will run at the same time.

3. Program Scene 1 – Bedroom1

The Princess slowly inches off her bed until she is standing upright. She then sends the **kidnap** broadcast making the Witch appear.

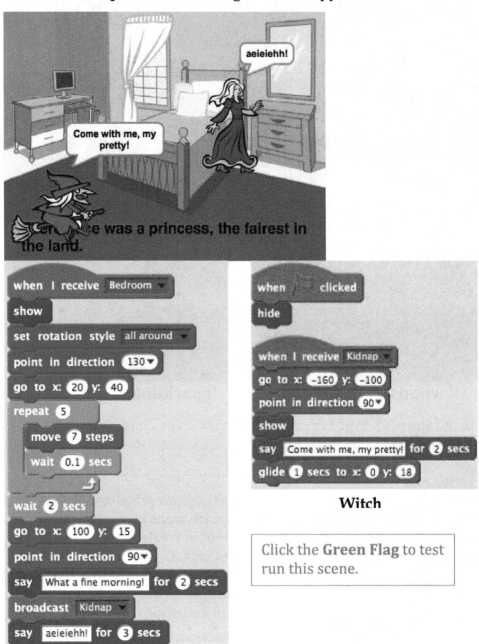

Witch

Click the **Green Flag** to test run this scene.

Princess

4. Program Scene 2 – Enter Prince

The Princess and Witch sprites vanish from the screen, and the Prince emerges from inside **castle1** by enlarging into view.

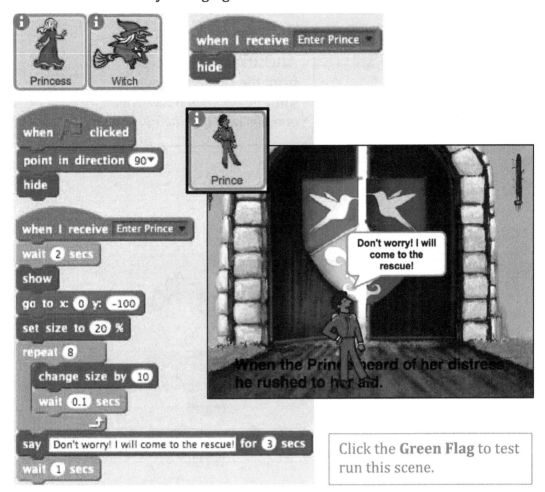

Click the **Green Flag** to test run this scene.

5. Program Scene 3 – Dark Forest

The Prince emerges from the castle, travels on the path, and stops. When the Bat2 sprite attacks him, the Prince sends him flying off the screen with a ninja kick.

Prince

```
when I receive Dark Forest ▼
go to x: -170 y: 15
set size to 20 %
repeat 8
    change size by 10
    change x by 10
repeat 8
    change x by 10
    change y by -10
wait until   touching Bat2 ▼ ?
repeat 6
    turn ↺ 20 degrees
say Hiyah! for 2 secs
wait 1 secs
point in direction 90▼
glide 1 secs to x: 240 y: -100
```

After the **Prince** emerges
from the castle, he waits
until he touches **Bat2**. This
enables him to time his kick.

Bat2

```
when ⚑ clicked
hide

when I receive Dark Forest ▼
wait 1 secs
set rotation style left-right ▼
go to x: 150 y: -20
show
repeat until   touching Prince ▼ ?
    next costume
    wait 0.1 secs
    move 10 steps
    point towards Prince ▼
glide 1 secs to x: -120 y: 180
hide
```

Bat2 constantly moves and points
towards **Prince** like a homing
missile. It touches the prince,
triggering his kick, and the bat
glides off the screen.

Click the **Green Flag** to test
run this scene.

6. Program Scene 4 – Fight the Dragon

The backdrop switches to **Woods,** and the Prince must use **Lightning** to fight the Dragon's **Fireballs**. Let's first program some instructions for the Prince. The game starts here.

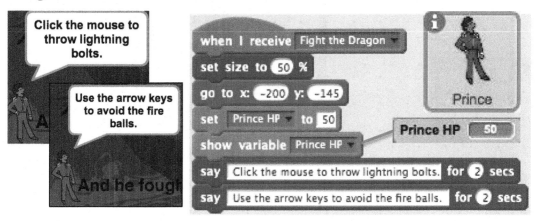

The following instruction blocks show how the Prince fires his Lightning bolts. If Prince gets hit 5 times by **Fireball**, his HP drops to 0. Make sure to create a **Prince HP** variable and a **Dragon HP** variable **for all sprites**.

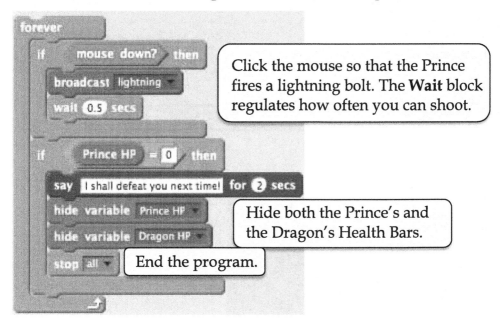

Now let's program the Prince's and Dragon's movement. The user moves the Prince around using the arrow keys. Meanwhile, the Dragon glides to random positions on the right side of the screen.

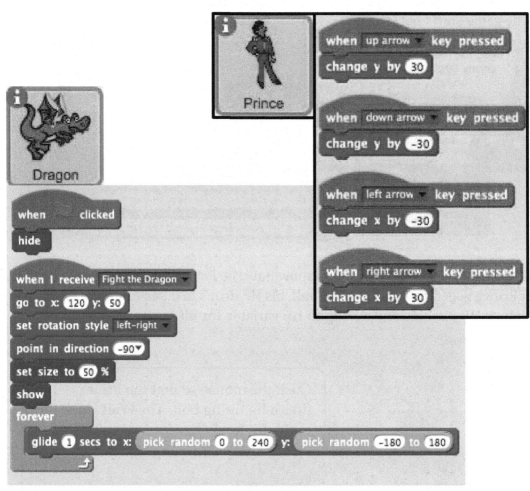

Let's program how we damage and slay the Dragon. Go to the **Dragon** sprite.

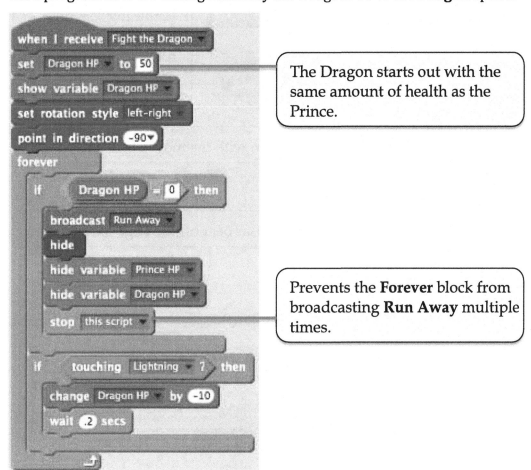

The Dragon starts out with the same amount of health as the Prince.

Prevents the **Forever** block from broadcasting **Run Away** multiple times.

Go to the **Lightning** sprite. Let's program the lightning bolts to appear when the Prince aims and fires with his mouse.

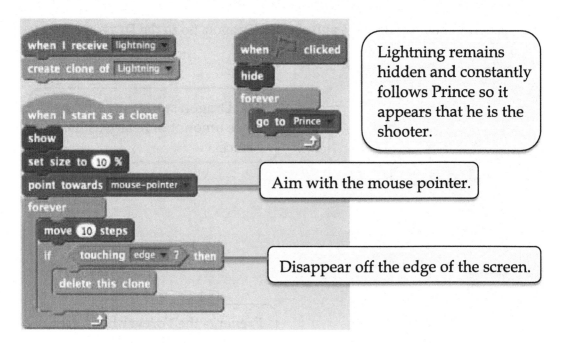

When I receive lightning
create clone of Lightning

when I start as a clone
show
set size to 10 %
point towards mouse-pointer
forever
  move 10 steps
  if touching edge ? then
    delete this clone

when [flag] clicked
hide
forever
  go to Prince

Lightning remains hidden and constantly follows Prince so it appears that he is the shooter.

Aim with the mouse pointer.

Disappear off the edge of the screen.

Let's to the same thing with the **Fireball** sprite.

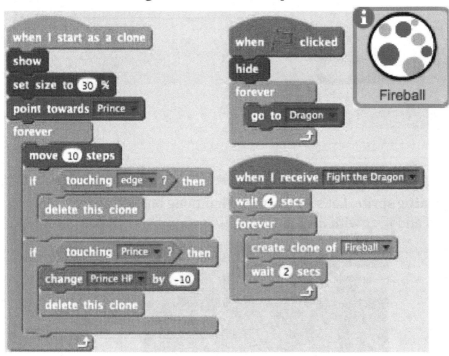

when I start as a clone
show
set size to 30 %
point towards Prince
forever
  move 10 steps
  if touching edge ? then
    delete this clone
  if touching Prince ? then
    change Prince HP by -10
    delete this clone

when [flag] clicked
hide
forever
  go to Dragon

Fireball

when I receive Fight the Dragon
wait 4 secs
forever
  create clone of Fireball
  wait 2 secs

Click the **Green Flag** to test run this scene.

7. Program Scene 5 – The End

If the Prince is defeated, the animation stops. But if the Dragon is defeated, **Run Away** is broadcasted, and the Witch temporarily appears to shout her defeat. Meanwhile, the Lightning and Fireball sprites stop creating clones.

During **The End** broadcast, the backdrop switches to **Sparkling**. The Princess declares the Prince her hero.

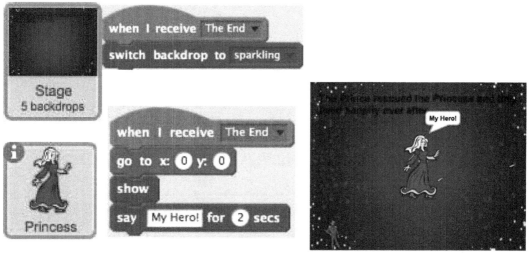

Click the **Green Flag,** and enjoy the animation!

Chapter 8 - Bitmap and Vector Paint Editor

Create a new project, and click the paintbrush symbol / to draw your own sprite. Next, go to the **Paint Editor** under the **Costumes** tab. Using the textbox, you can name each costume.

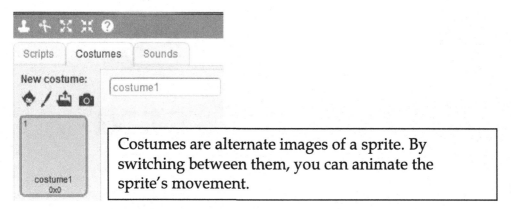

Costumes are alternate images of a sprite. By switching between them, you can animate the sprite's movement.

Here is a close-up of the **Paint Editor**. There are two interchangeable modes: **Bitmap** and **Vector**. **Bitmap** is the default but you can switch to **Vector** by clicking the **Convert to Vector** button on the bottom-right hand corner.

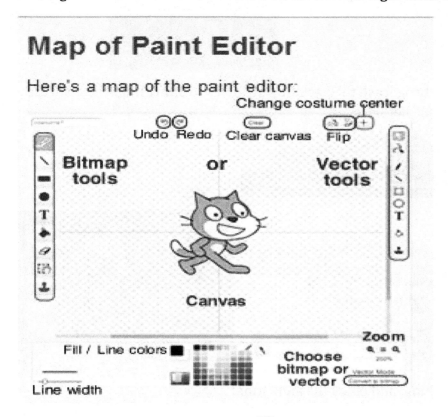

Draw a Green Apple in Vector Mode

If you are in **Bitmap Mode**, click Convert to vector to convert to **Vector Mode**.

Here is a brief summary of the Vector Paint Tools:

Once you are familiar with the Vector tools, let's start drawing a green apple.

1. Select green from your color palette.

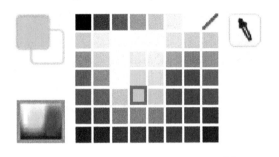

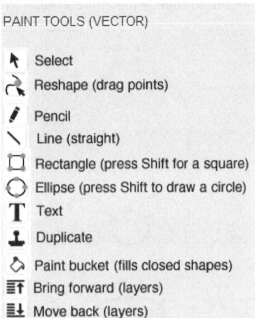

PAINT TOOLS (VECTOR)

↖	Select
↻	Reshape (drag points)
✏	Pencil
↘	Line (straight)
▭	Rectangle (press Shift for a square)
◯	Ellipse (press Shift to draw a circle)
T	Text
⊥	Duplicate
◇	Paint bucket (fills closed shapes)
☰↑	Bring forward (layers)
☰↓	Move back (layers)
▪	Group
▪	Ungroup

2. Select the **Ellipse**(Oval) tool ◯. Make sure the oval isn't filled and its line width isn't too thick or thin. Then, draw an oval as shown below.

3. Use the **Duplicate** tool ⊥ to make a copy of the oval.

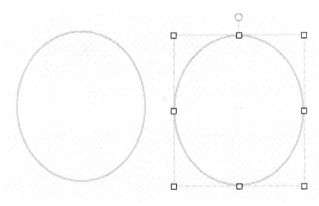

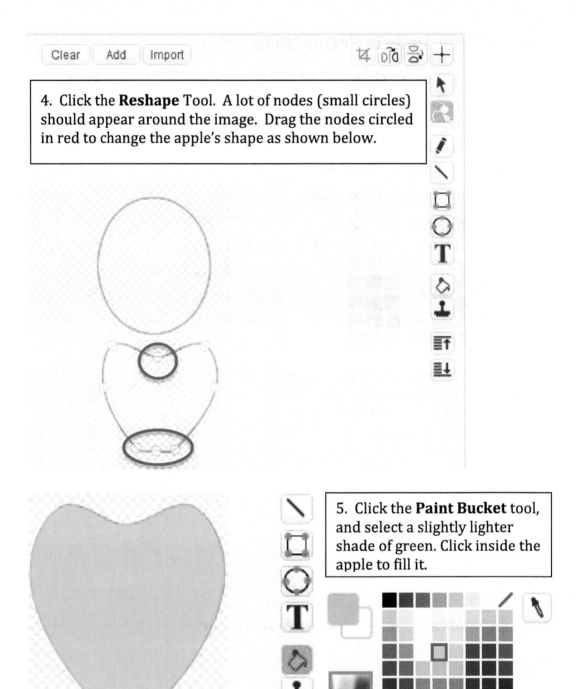

4. Click the **Reshape** Tool. A lot of nodes (small circles) should appear around the image. Drag the nodes circled in red to change the apple's shape as shown below.

5. Click the **Paint Bucket** tool, and select a slightly lighter shade of green. Click inside the apple to fill it.

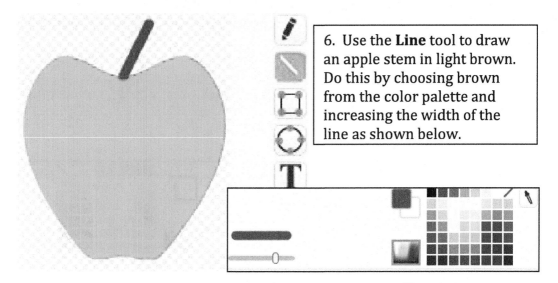

6. Use the **Line** tool to draw an apple stem in light brown. Do this by choosing brown from the color palette and increasing the width of the line as shown below.

7. Let's give the apple a gradient to reflect the light. Select ◇. Choose the primary color by clicking apple green ▯, and make the secondary color yellow ▯. Then select the highlighted option below, and fill your apple with this gradient.

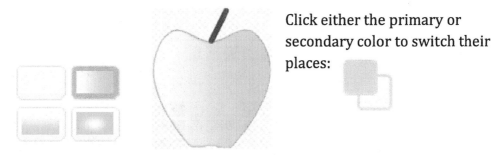

Click either the primary or secondary color to switch their places:

8. Use the **Select** tool to highlight both the apple and it's stem. Then, click the **Group** button. Now, changes apply to both the apple and stem as a whole. Click the duplicate button to make another copy of the apple.

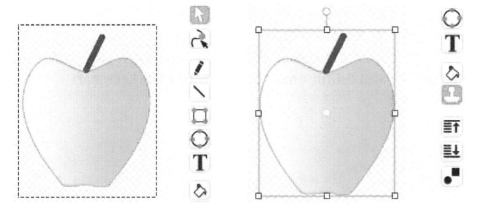

9. Fill the duplicated apple with white. Make sure that the no-gradient option is selected.

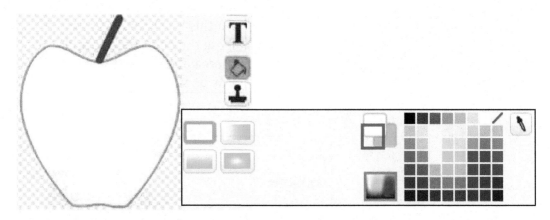

10. Use the **Ellipse** tool ⬭ to draw four dark brown seeds inside the apple.

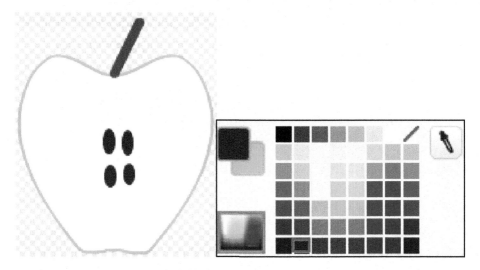

Congratulations! You drew your first sprite!

Draw a Girl's Face in Vector Mode

Create a new project, and click the paintbrush symbol / to draw your own sprite. Next, go to the **Paint Editor** under the **Costumes** tab. Let's start drawing the girl's curly hair.

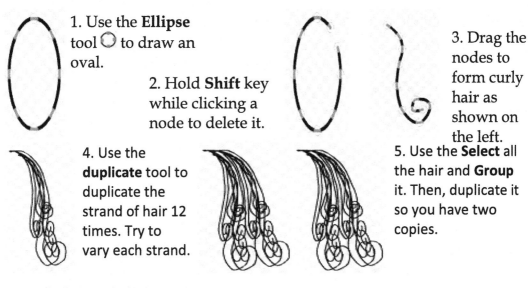

1. Use the **Ellipse** tool ⊘ to draw an oval.

2. Hold **Shift** key while clicking a node to delete it.

3. Drag the nodes to form curly hair as shown on the left.

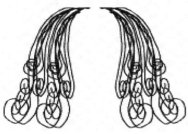

4. Use the **duplicate** tool to duplicate the strand of hair 12 times. Try to vary each strand.

5. Use the **Select** all the hair and **Group** it. Then, duplicate it so you have two copies.

6. Use the **Flip** button ▯ on the upper-right corner to flip one set of hair.

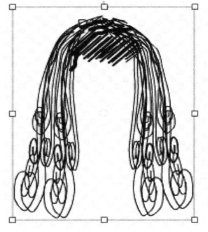

7. Connect the two groups of hair together. Then, use the ⟍ multiple times to add bangs.

8. Now let's draw the face. Use ⊘, ⟍, and ◇ to draw the shapes below. Let's first reshape the eyebrows with ⌒. 1) Click ⌒ and select the line. 2) Create two nodes by clicking two times in the middle of the eyebrow. 3) Drag the end nodes slightly downwards.

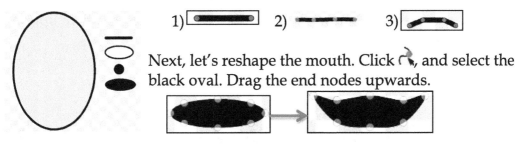

1) 2) 3)

Next, let's reshape the mouth. Click ⌒, and select the black oval. Drag the end nodes upwards.

The eyes are simple. 1) Drag the black circle into the white oval. 2) Use  to group them together. 3) Duplicate the eye with , and put all of your facial features together. 4) Group your facial features, and put them on the face.

Use 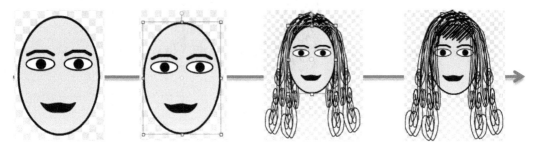 to group the face with its parts. Then, drag the face in front of the hair. Click to shift the face back layers until the hair appears in front of it.

Draw a Windsurfer in Bitmap Mode

1. Let's draw the background. First, start with the ocean. Use 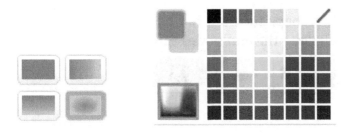 to draw the waves.

> Make sure the waves touch both sides. If there are any gaps, then ✦ will fill the whole screen instead of just the waves.

2. Now let's add color. Click the paint can, and choose the primary and secondary colors shown below. Then, select the bottom-left gradient option.

Fill the wave with this gradient several times.

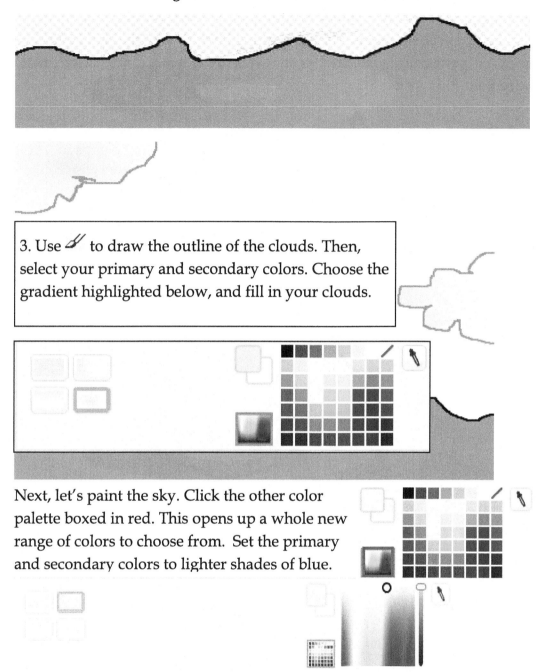

3. Use ✎ to draw the outline of the clouds. Then, select your primary and secondary colors. Choose the gradient highlighted below, and fill in your clouds.

Next, let's paint the sky. Click the other color palette boxed in red. This opens up a whole new range of colors to choose from. Set the primary and secondary colors to lighter shades of blue.

Fill in the white background with the highlighted gradient.

Now let's draw the windsurfer, starting with the board. Select the color ▮, use ⊘, and select the filled circle option to draw a surfboard. Then, rotate it at an angle as shown below. Use ↘ to draw the outline of the sail. Follow the order for drawing your lines as shown below. Finally, draw a circle in the center.

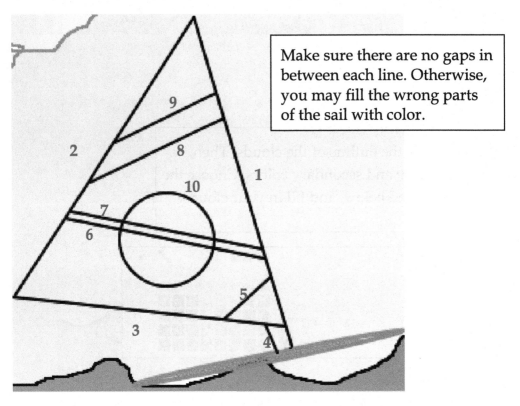

Make sure there are no gaps in between each line. Otherwise, you may fill the wrong parts of the sail with color.

Next, fill each part of the sail with color.

Which Mode should You Use?

The vector graphics improve the graphic quality of your images because of its greater clarity and resolution. It also offers flexibility to layer different objects on top of each other and allows the ease of future changes. Vector graphics use nodes that can be dragged to transform a shape, so getting the right shape is much easier. Objects can also be manipulated individually so you can stretch and rotate an element separately or change elements collectively. You can also reuse some components in different costumes with only minor changes to one or two components. For example, if you draw a person talking, the only change you may have to make is to the mouth or eyelids. The backdrop and the rest of the body may stay the same. Vector is many people's favorite drawing mode.

The bitmap editor can fill any enclosed area with color as long as the area is enclosed with lines and the edge of the draw area. The vector editor can only fill in enclosed areas drawn with end points of the lines meet. It cannot fill in the color for the above Windsurfer waves or the clouds. It also has an **Erase** tool that's very handy when you want erase something from the image.

Note: When you convert **Vector Mode** into **Bitmap Mode**, you can no longer switch back to make changes to individual lines or shapes drawn in **Vector Mode**.

Chapter 9 – People Sprites

In this chapter, we will animate human sprites. You will learn how to make stick figures walk, blink, and talk.

1. Walking Sprite (Drawing with Vector Mode)

Create a new project, **Walking Sprite**. Then, let's draw some costumes to emulate the walking motion. Click ✏, and name the sprite, **Walking Sprite.** Go to the paint editor, and switch it to **Vector Mode** so you can move around body parts more easily. The costumes below illustrate the walking motion:

Let's draw **Walking Sprite's** first costume. Use ＼ and ↻ to draw the limbs and ○ to draw the head as shown below. When you make the arms and legs with multiple lines, group the line segments together with •▪:

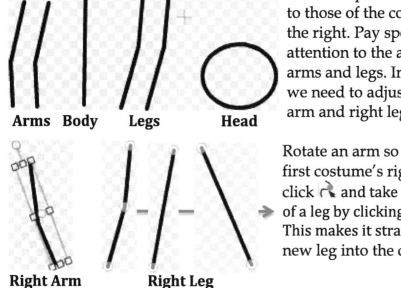

Arms Body   Legs   Head

Right Arm   Right Leg

Now compare the body parts to those of the costume on the right. Pay special attention to the angle of the arms and legs. In this case, we need to adjust the right arm and right leg.

Rotate an arm so it looks like the first costume's right arm. Next, click ↻ and take out the center joint of a leg by clicking the center node. This makes it straight. Rotate this new leg into the costume's right leg.

Now that we have the right arms and legs, let's arrange everything together.

The first costume is finished! Now let's duplicate it 4 times to create the next 4 costumes. Repeat this process in order to create the other costumes:

1. Take apart the body parts, and arrange them in an organized line.
2. Compare each arm and leg to respective limbs of the costume at the beginning of this chapter.
3. Adjust the tilt of the limbs that don't match.
4. Once every body part mimics those of each costume, put them back together.

This saves time and ensures that each costume is similar in size. If you aren't able to draw these costumes to your liking, you can download them by going to Ch. 9 in our online resources and importing **Walking Sprite.sprite2.**

Now let's make **Walking Sprite** walk.

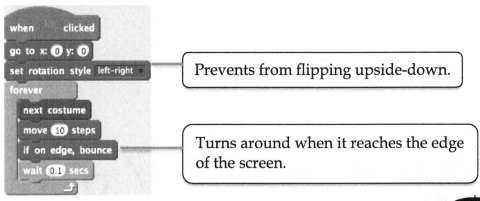

Prevents from flipping upside-down.

Turns around when it reaches the edge of the screen.

If you drew your own costumes, you may notice that **Walking Sprite** doesn't walk evenly. It's costumes may be off-center. If so, go to each of your costumes, and click +. Click at the point where both arms connect to the body. This centers the costume.

Click the **Green Flag** to test run this scene.

2. Blinking Sprite (Drawing with Bitmap Mode)

Blinking makes a person or an animal come alive. This is the easiest way to animate. Create a new project called, **Blinking Sprite.** Click ✏, and rename the sprite, **Blinking Sprite.** Then, go to the paint editor, and make sure it's in **Bitmap Mode**.

1. Draw the Basic Face

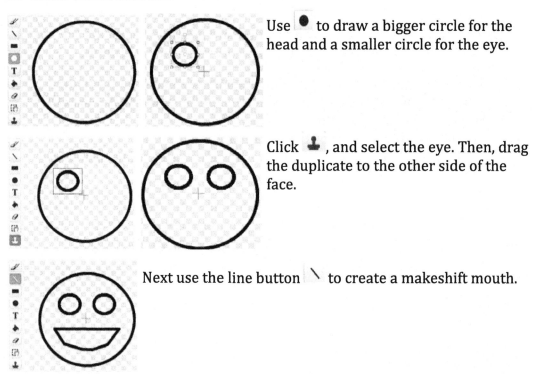

Use ● to draw a bigger circle for the head and a smaller circle for the eye.

Click ⚓, and select the eye. Then, drag the duplicate to the other side of the face.

Next use the line button ＼ to create a makeshift mouth.

2. Draw Blinking Costumes

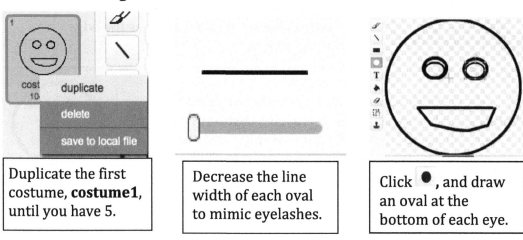

Duplicate the first costume, **costume1**, until you have 5.

Decrease the line width of each oval to mimic eyelashes.

Click ●, and draw an oval at the bottom of each eye.

The space in between the two ovals is the eyelash. Once you finished giving the first costume eyelashes, do the same for the other costumes. The inner ovals in **costume2** and **costume3** should gradually decrease in height. For **costume4**, use ＼ to draw a line on the bottom of the eye. This makes the eyelid seem closed.

| costume2 | costume3 | costume4 |

3. Program the Face

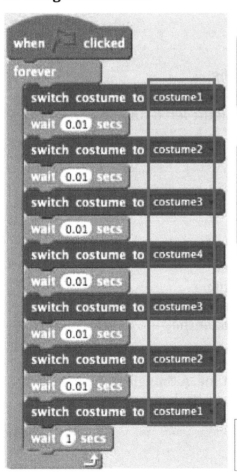

The **Wait** blocks set the speed of each blink. The last **Wait** block sets the time interval in between each blink.

Notice that the costumes are ordered 1234321. This allows us to see the eyes gradually open back up after blinking. If we used the **Next Costume** block, it would set the costume order to 12341234...

Click the **Green Flag** to test run this scene.

3. Talking Sprite

Create a new project called, **Talking Sprite.** Then click ✏, and rename the new sprite, **Talking Sprite.** Now let's go to the paint editor in **Bitmap Mode**.

1. Add the Basic Face

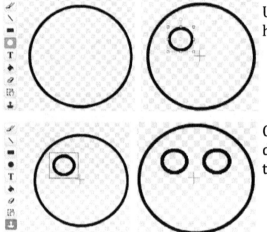

Use ● to draw a bigger circle for the head and a smaller circle for the eye.

Click ⬇, and highlight the eye. Then, drag the duplicate to the other side of the face.

2. Create 9 Faces, each with Specific Mouths

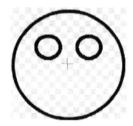

Duplicate the costume on the left **8 times**.

We will add a different mouth to each costume starting with **costume1**. Go to the paint editor and click Import. Choose the picture, **A.png,** from Ch. 9 in our online resources. Resize mouth to fit the face and place it below the eyes. Make sure the costume is named, **A**, after the sound that it makes.

A

If you look closely, each mouth has a white outline. Although, this won't show up against a white background, it will for colored backgrounds. Let's remove this white space.

1. Click the paint can
2. Choose the transparent color ╱.
3. Remove the white space.

> Note: Each mouth is named after the sounds it represents. For example, the mouth, BMP, represents the B, M, and P sounds.

Import the remaining mouth pictures from Ch. 9 in our online resources into your costumes, and repeat the previous steps for each costume.

3. Program the Mouth to Talk

Let's have our mouth say the name, "Beverly".

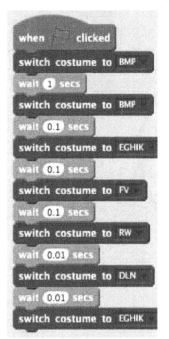

> Start with the costume, BMP, because this is the mouth's resting position.

> Split the name into syllables. In this case, Beverly is split into B-E-V-R-L-E. We replaced "er" with R and "y" with E because the mouth moves according to pronunciation and not spelling.

> The **Switch Costume** blocks specify the appropriate costume. The **Wait** blocks regulate the mouth's talking speed.

To produce sound, we have to lip sync the mouth with a sound recording. Go to the **Sounds** tab, click 🎤 to record a new sound, and name it **Beverly**. Before you do anything else, **increase your microphone volume.**

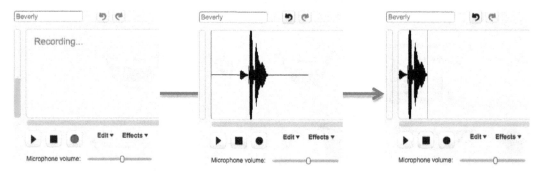

Otherwise, your computer won't pick up your voice.

Now we can start recording. Click ⏺ to begin. To end this sound recording, click ⏹.

Replay the sound by clicking ▶. There probably is a brief pause at the beginning and end of the recording. The flat line on the graph signifies this silence. Use your mouse to highlight the flat lines at the beginning and end. Delete them with the **delete/backspace** key or click **Edit > delete**.

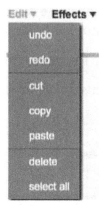

Now let's insert the sound, Beverly, into our scripts:

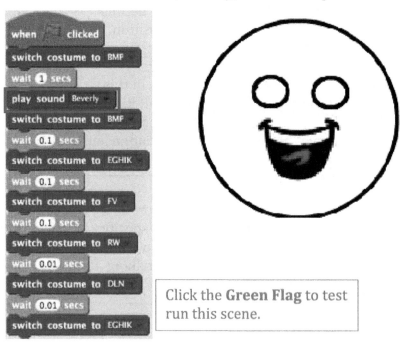

Click the **Green Flag** to test run this scene.

68

Chapter 10 - Nature Simulation Techniques

This chapter creates settings for your animation. It gives life to any story. We will introduce a few techniques for your use, and when you understand how nature can be simulated, you can simulate your own.

1. Animate Rain

Create a new Scratch project called, **Rain**, and create a **Rain** sprite. It can look like a dot or a drop. Then, let's program this sprite to create rain clones that fall to the bottom of the screen and disappear.

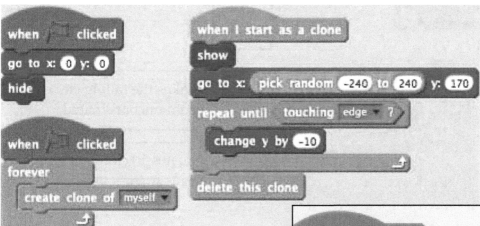

Go to the **Stage's Backdrops** tab, and open the paint editor. Make sure you are in **Vector** mode. Click T, and type "**Dance in the Rain**" in red.

Dance in the Rain

Program this backdrop to swirl around and reset every 6 seconds with the code on the right.

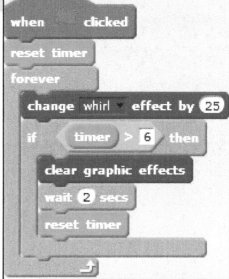

Click the **Green Flag** to test run this scene.

69

2. Animate Rain Splashing on the Umbrella on a Windy Day

Create a new project called, **Splashing Rain**. First, click 📤, and go to Ch. 10 in our online resources. Choose **Umbrella.sprite2** and **Rain.sprite2**. When rain lands on the umbrella, it splatters ✸✸✸ by switching costumes. The umbrella doesn't need any programming.

Now let's program the **Rain** sprite on a windy day. Make sure to create a variable "**wind**".

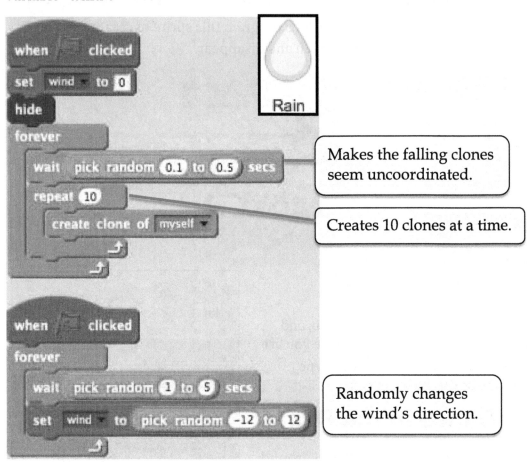

Makes the falling clones seem uncoordinated.

Creates 10 clones at a time.

Randomly changes the wind's direction.

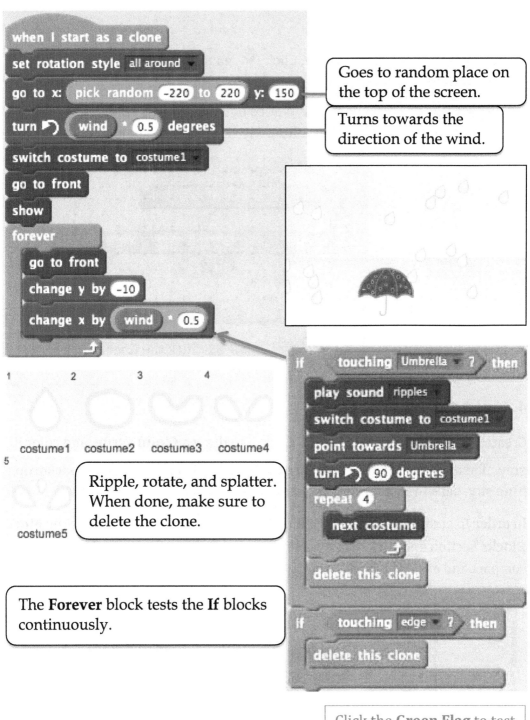

when I start as a clone

set rotation style all around ▾

go to x: pick random -220 to 220 y: 150

> Goes to random place on the top of the screen.

turn ↻ wind * 0.5 degrees

> Turns towards the direction of the wind.

switch costume to costume1 ▾

go to front

show

forever

  go to front

  change y by -10

  change x by wind * 0.5

1   2   3   4

costume1 costume2 costume3 costume4

5

costume5

> Ripple, rotate, and splatter. When done, make sure to delete the clone.

if touching Umbrella ▾ ? then

  play sound ripples

  switch costume to costume1

  point towards Umbrella ▾

  turn ↻ 90 degrees

  repeat 4

    next costume

  delete this clone

if touching edge ▾ ? then

  delete this clone

> The **Forever** block tests the **If** blocks continuously.

> Click the **Green Flag** to test run this scene.

71

3. Animate Snow

Create a new project called, **Snow**. Click , go to the **Holiday** theme, and add **snowflake**.

Snowflake

Now let's program each snowflake. Notice how this code is similar to the **Rain** sprite's code, but the snowflakes fall slowly since they are lighter.

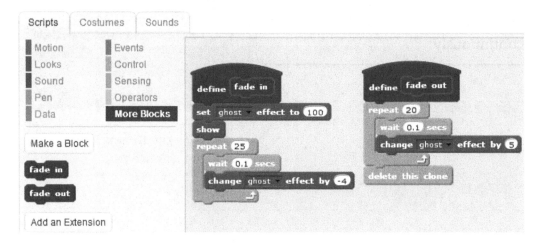

Click the **Green Flag** to test run this scene.

4. Animate Clouds

Create a new project called, **Cloud**. Click ✏ to draw a **Cloud** sprite, and color it gray. Then, go to the **Stage Backdrop** tab. Click 🖼 and choose the backdrop, **blue sky**. Let's first create procedures for each cloud clone.

In order to create the **Procedure** blocks **Fade In** and **Fade Out**, go to the **More Blocks** section and click `Make a Block`. Procedure blocks make the code more compact and easier to read. They save you from duplicating blocks.

Once you define these procedures, new procedure blocks should appear in the menu. Now let's create the Cloud clones and program them.

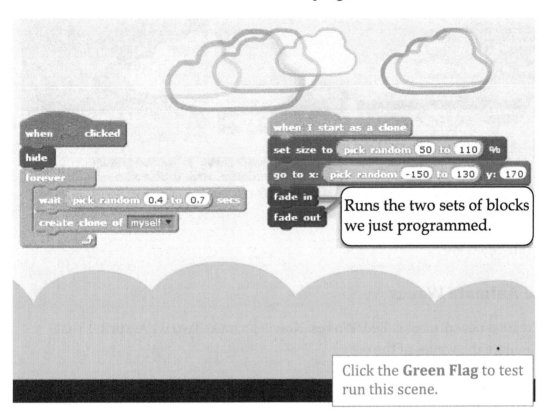

Runs the two sets of blocks we just programmed.

Click the **Green Flag** to test run this scene.

5. Animate Wind

Go to Ch. 10 in our online resources and open **Wind.sb2**. Because wind is invisible, use other objects to show that wind is present.

Use the following code to animate each tree sprite and thereby to animate wind.

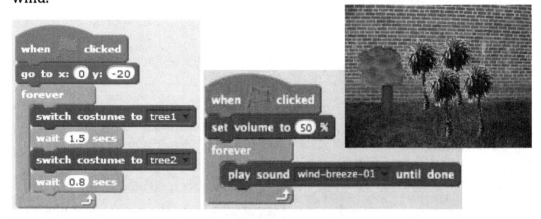

> Click the **Green Flag** to test run this scene.

6. Animate Waves

Create a new project called, **Waves**. Now let's make two wave sprites that simulate the waves of the ocean.

Create **Wave1** by clicking ✏. Go to the paint editor and use the line button ╲ to create a series of zig-zagging lines acrose the screen.

Then, fill the wave with blue ■ using 🔵. Make sure the lines are all connected. If there is a small gap, 🔵 would fill the whole screen.

After you created your first wave sprite, duplicate it into **Wave2**. The only change you need to make is to use 🔵 to fill the wave with a slightly darker shade of blue ■.

Now let's program each wave sprite. Notice how similar they are. You can duplicate **Wave1's** blocks and make some minor changes to produce **Wave2's** blocks.

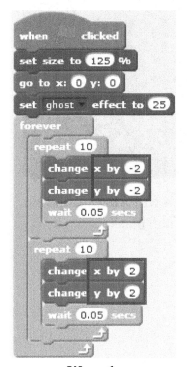

Wave1

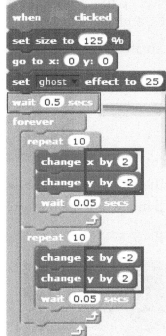

Wave2

Delays the zigzag motion to prevent the waves from overlapping.

Notice the x and y values change to shift the wave sideways, up, and down.

Click the **Green Flag** to test run this scene.

Chapter 11 - Theatrical Effects

This chapter provides you tools to create a sense of mystery, suspense, and surprise. We will animate a flash of lightning and a shaking face. These projects utilize the theatrical effects of brightness, ghost, zoom in, and shake.

1. Animate Lightning and Thunder

First, create a new project, **Lightning Flash,** and delete the cat sprite. Go to Ch. 11 in our online resources, and click  to import the **Lightning** sprite.

Next, go to the **Stage**'s **Backdrops** tab. Select the default white backdrop, and make sure you are in **Bitmap** mode. Fill the background in black.

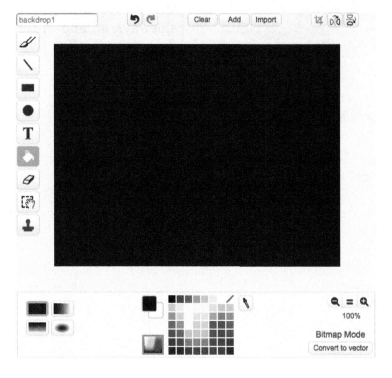

Next, go to your **Lightning** sprite.

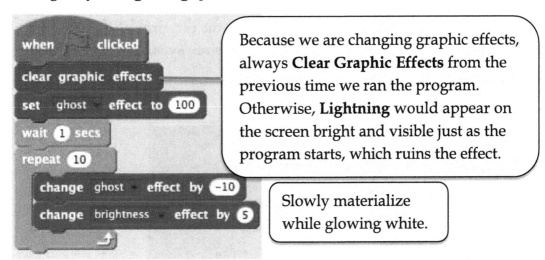

when [flag] clicked
clear graphic effects
set ghost effect to 100
wait 1 secs
repeat 10
  change ghost effect by -10
  change brightness effect by 5

Because we are changing graphic effects, always **Clear Graphic Effects** from the previous time we ran the program. Otherwise, **Lightning** would appear on the screen bright and visible just as the program starts, which ruins the effect.

Slowly materialize while glowing white.

Now let's program the lightning flash to fade away.

repeat 5
  change ghost effect by 20
  change brightness effect by -10

Go to the **Sound** tab, and click ⬆ to import **thunder.wav** from Ch. 11 in our online resources. Insert the sound so it runs while we are adjusting **Lightning's** graphic effects.

y: 0

when [flag] clicked
clear graphic effects
set ghost effect to 100
wait 1 secs
play sound thunder
repeat 10
  change ghost effect by -10
  change brightness effect by 5
repeat 5
  change ghost effect by 20
  change brightness effect by -10

Click the **Green Flag** to test run this scene.

77

2. Animate a Nervous Face

Create a new project, **Shaking Face**, and delete the cat sprite. Go to Ch. 11 in our online resources, and click 🖥 to import **Nervous Eyes.png**.

Go **Nervous Eyes'** paint editor; notice that the picture doesn't cover the whole width of the screen.

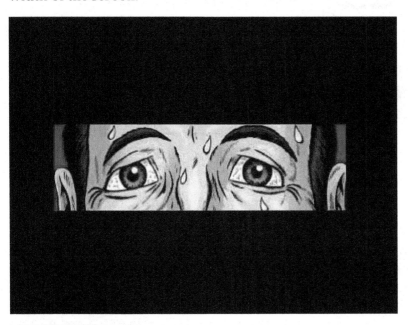

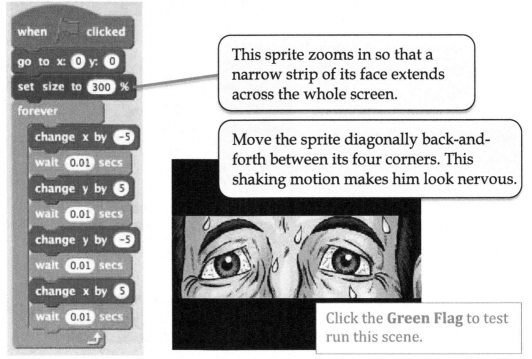

This sprite zooms in so that a narrow strip of its face extends across the whole screen.

Move the sprite diagonally back-and-forth between its four corners. This shaking motion makes him look nervous.

Click the **Green Flag** to test run this scene.

Chapter 12 - Layering Technique

Layering ensures that your animations look real and sophisticated. They could also prevent big sprites from blocking smaller sprites from view.

First, go to Ch. 12 in our online resources, and open **Merry Go Round Layering – Blank.sb2**. Go to the **Center** sprite and add a **Go To** block to keep it centered.

Next, go to the **Top** sprite, which contains two similar costumes of alternating blue and green color.

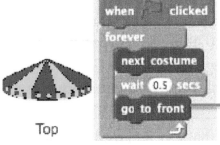

Top

This block gives **Top** the highest priority visibility.

The sensor sprites provide a reference point for the rider sprites. They must be visible so they are painted red in order to blend into the platform. Add the blocks to the sensor sprites below:

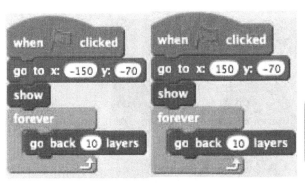

Sensor1   Sensor2

Constantly go to the back so they don't appear when rider sprites glide over them.

Now let's go to **Rider1** and program his motion on the Merry-Go-Round.

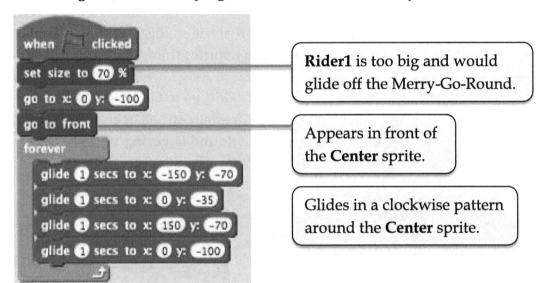

Rider1 is too big and would glide off the Merry-Go-Round.

Appears in front of the **Center** sprite.

Glides in a clockwise pattern around the **Center** sprite.

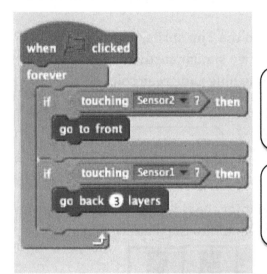

Riders that touch **Sensor2** after emerging from behind **Center** are given higher layering priority.

Riders that touch **Sensor1** after gliding in front of the **Center** sprite are given lower priority.

Behind

In front

Duplicate **Rider1's** motion blocks, and move the copies to **Rider2**, **Rider3**, and **Rider4**. The four riders have similar programming. Only minor changes need to be made to each sprite's initial position and gliding pathway.

Adjust each set of blocks with the respective values designated for each sprite.

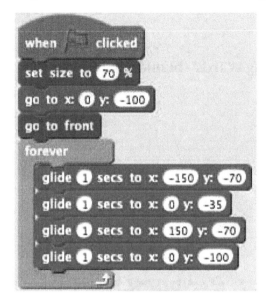

Rider1

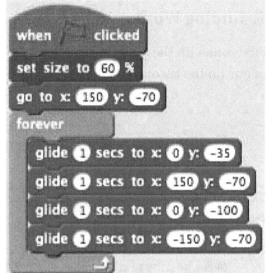

Rider2

when clicked
set size to 70 %
go to x: 0 y: -35
forever
    glide 1 secs to x: 150 y: -70
    glide 1 secs to x: 0 y: -100
    glide 1 secs to x: -150 y: -70
    glide 1 secs to x: 0 y: -35

Rider3

when clicked
go to x: -150 y: -70
forever
    glide 1 secs to x: 0 y: -100
    glide 1 secs to x: -150 y: -70
    glide 1 secs to x: 0 y: -35
    glide 1 secs to x: 150 y: -70

Rider4

Now let's click the **Green Flag**, and enjoy the animation!

Chapter 13 - Word and Letter Techniques

Words can be animated like any other typical sprites. They focus the audience's attention on the message. In this chapter, we'll introduce a few techniques for you to apply to your own programs.

1. Gliding Words

First, open up the Scratch Template, **Gliding Words - blank.sb2**, from Ch. 13 in our online resources.

Click the **DemoSlide** sprite and add the code below:

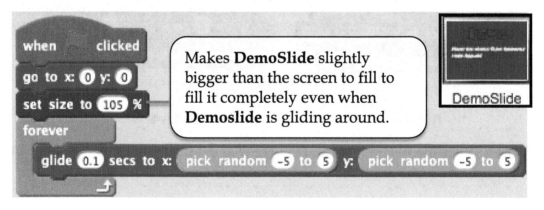

Makes **DemoSlide** slightly bigger than the screen to fill to fill it completely even when **Demoslide** is gliding around.

The gliding words of **DemoSlide** produce the greatest effect when presented with other animated sprites. In this case, let's make our **SpinningO** sprite spin!

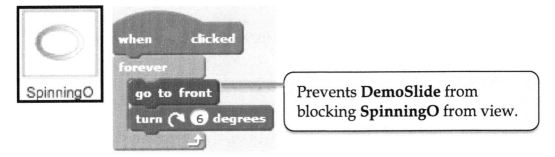

Prevents **DemoSlide** from blocking **SpinningO** from view.

Now let's have the **SlideIn** sprite slide in when the spacebar is pressed.

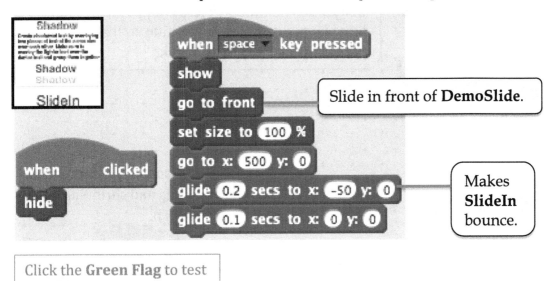

Slide in front of **DemoSlide**.

Makes **SlideIn** bounce.

Click the **Green Flag** to test run this scene.

2. Zooming Words

Create a new project called **Zooming Words**, and delete the cat sprite. Next, click ✎ to paint your own sprite. Go to the paint editor's **vector** mode, click 🎨, and type in "Game Over" in red. Then, rename this sprite, **ZoomInAndOut**.

Game Over

Now let's use this sprite to demonstrate different zooming tricks. Each trick will appear when a certain letter on the keyboard is pressed. For now, let's go to the **Scripts** tab.

First, let's slightly grow and shrink **ZoomInAndOut** 4 times when we press a.

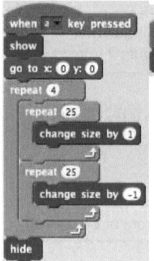

Changing size by the smallest increment makes this zoom effect less choppy. It also slows down each repetition so that we don't need any **Wait** blocks.

Second, let's zoom out of this sprite by making it big and shrinking it when we press b.

Third, let's zoom in to this sprite by making this it small and enlargening it when we press c.

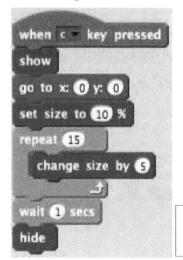
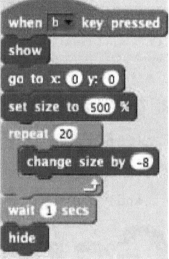

Click the **Green Flag** to test run this scene.

3. Listing Letters

Create a new project called **Listing Letters.** In this animation, the starting cat sprite speaks by adding one letter at a time to its original sentence. Here are a couple examples:

This animation uses lists, which are tools that store multiple items at once. To create a list, go to the **Data** section and click Make a List. Name the list, "**Welcome**", and stick with the default list setting, **For all sprites**

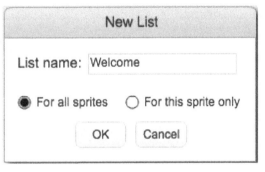

Like adding variables, adding lists makes a whole set of **Data** blocks available. Let's create a list at the start of the program.

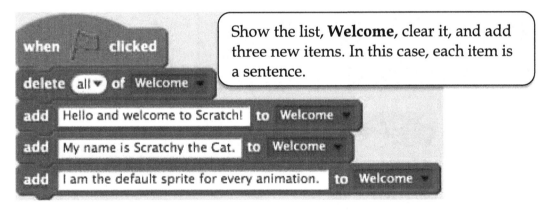

Show the list, **Welcome**, clear it, and add three new items. In this case, each item is a sentence.

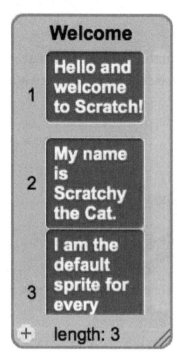

Each sentence is paired with a number that shows whether the item is first, second, or third in the list. Items can be added, deleted, or read from the list to run the program.

Next, create three variables named, **Sentence**, **letter**, and **item**. We will keep track of these variables throughout the program. Now we should set their starting values. Add these blocks to the bottom of the script:

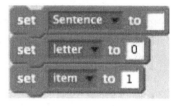

Now let's process the first **Item** in the **Welcome** list and program the cat to say it letter by letter.

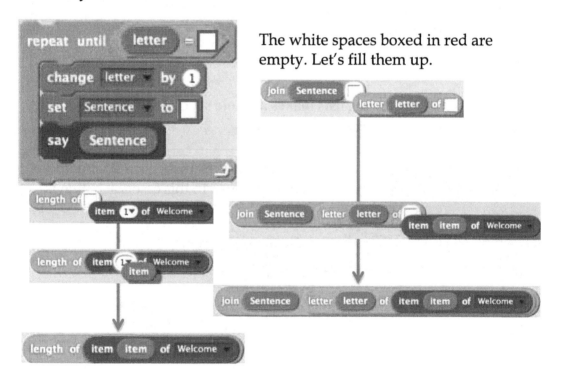

The white spaces boxed in red are empty. Let's fill them up.

Add these two sets of **Operator** blocks into the red boxes as shown above.

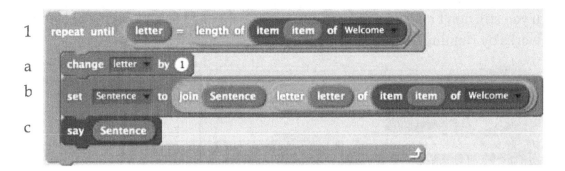

1. **Repeat until** the cat is on the last letter in the first(**item**=1) sentence of the list.
   a. Move on to the next letter that has yet to be added.
   b. Add this letter to **Sentence.**
   c. **Say Sentence**

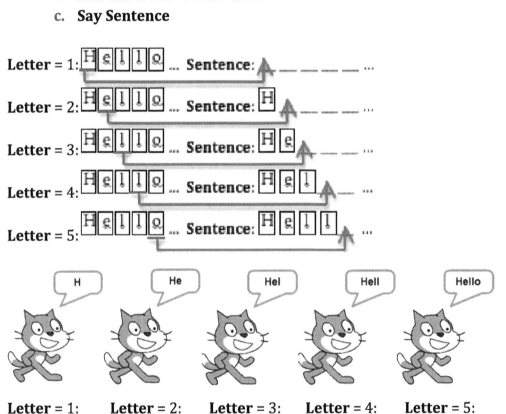

Letter = 1: **Letter = 2:** **Letter = 3:** **Letter = 4:** **Letter = 5:**

87

If you still don't understand, combine your scripts and learn how the program works by running it.

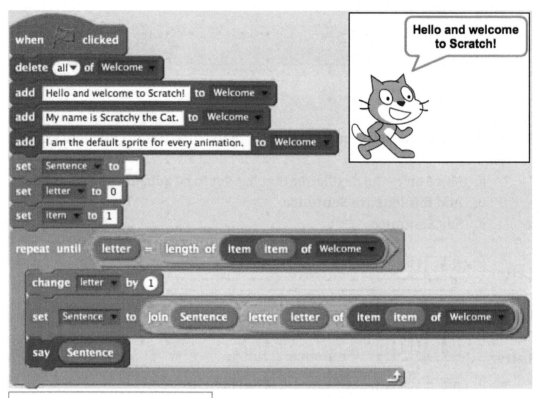

Click the **Green Flag** to test run this scene.

Chapter 14 - Scrolling Sprite Techniques

Scrolling Sprites give the ground and background cinematic effects. There are two types of scrolling: Vertical and Horizontal. We will introduce a few techniques in both categories for you to use.

1. Animate Messages with Vertical Scrolling

First, go to Ch. 14 in our online resources, and open **Message Vertical Scroll – Blank.sb2**. This Scratch project already contains the background and the **Message** sprite. Click the **Message** sprite and add:

Message

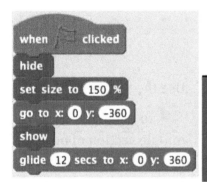

Make sure you do your homework or you will be grounded for a week. :3

> This sprite already covers the screen from top to bottom. **Set Size to 150 %** creates a zoomed-in effect. The message then starts on the bottom of the screen and glides to the top until it is mostly out of view.

This technique can be used to show closing credits like those at the end of any movie. You can also present a written message on the screen in this scrolling fashion.

> Click the **Green Flag** to test run this scene.

2. Animate a Winding River with Vertical Scrolling

Create a new project, **River Vertical Scroll**. Click ✏ to draw a winding river sprite, and delete the cat sprite. Name this sprite **River1**. Then, go to the paint editor of the **River1** sprite, and choose the **Line** tool ◥ in the **Bitmap** editor.

 In the bottom left-hand corner of the editor, adjust the line width by moving the slider to the middle.

Make sure the **Bitmap** editor is zoomed in **100%** so you can see the white sprite on the screen. Select the color **black** from the color palette.

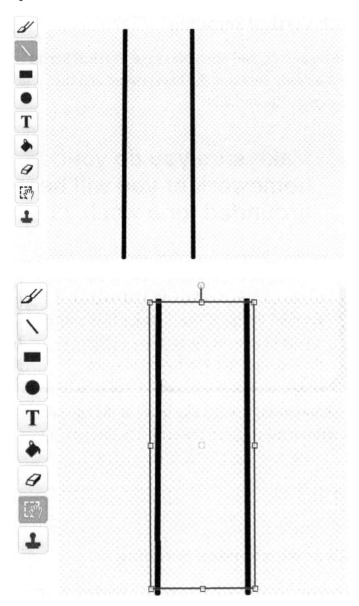

Draw two STRAIGHT, vertical lines on your screen. Make sure that they TOUCH the top and bottom of the paint editor. Otherwise, the **Fill With Color** button will not work properly.

Use the **Select** button to highlight the middle section of both lines, leaving out the upper and lower tips. Delete this selected section so that two pairs of two dots remain on the top and bottom of the screen.

Duplicate this sprite , which consists of two sets of dots, 3 times. Rename these sprites **River2**, **River3**, and **River4**. Now, we have 4 river templates.

Go to **River1** and draw the side of the river that is closest to the edge. Use the **Paintbrush** button 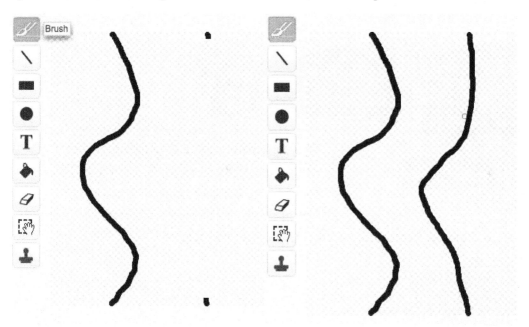 to connect the leftmost and rightmost dots on the top and bottom with winding lines. If possible, try to leave a reasonable amount of space in between each part of the line to mimic the shape of a river.

Now, select the **Fill With Color** button 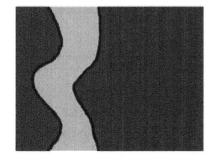 and select the darkest shade of brown ■. Click both sides of the river to fill the banks with mud. Next, set the color to a lighter shade of blue ■, and fill in the river.

Now that you have created the **river1** sprite, use the same process to draw the other three river sprites. If you want, you can customize both of the muddy banks lying beside the riverside with plants and animals.

By now, you should have four river sprites ready to program.

River1

River2

River3

River4

Notice that each river sprite begins and ends at the same position on the screen. This allows us to arrange each sprite on top of the other. This creates one long, continuous river.

Now let's program each sprite. Click the **River1** sprite, and create the variable **ScrollY, for all sprites.**

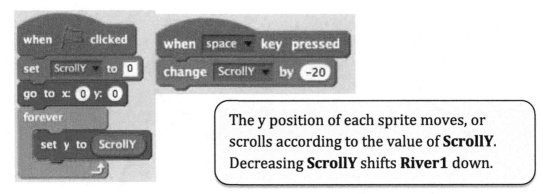

The y position of each sprite moves, or scrolls according to the value of **ScrollY**. Decreasing **ScrollY** shifts **River1** down.

Insert the blocks boxed in red into the **Forever** block.

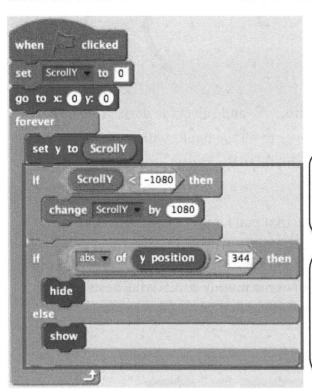

Continually test when to shift **River1** back to the top of the screen.

Each river sprite can't move completely off the screen. We must hide them when their **y positions** exceed a certain point.

Next, let's program the other three river sprites. Their code is similar to each other except for one minor detail. Right click the set of blocks in the figure above and duplicate it. Drag and drop these blocks onto **River2**. Then, go to the **River2** sprite to view them.

Delete the portions crossed out in red. Because **ScrollY** is the same for all sprites, a change in **ScrollY** within the scripts of the **River1** sprite changes **ScrollY** for the other river sprites.

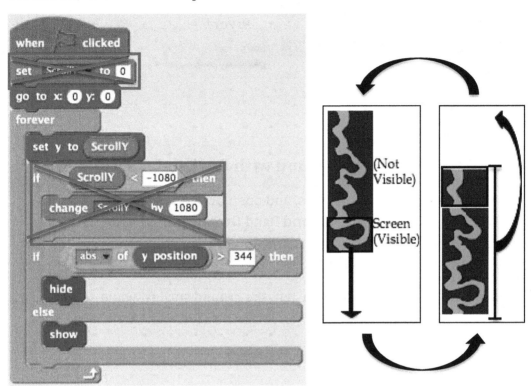

Next, duplicate **River2's** remaining blocks and drag-and-drop them into **River3** and **River4**. Replace the boxed blocks in **River2**, **River3**, and **River4** with the blocks shown below. This stacks the river sprites on top of each other to create a continuous river. Notice that each consecutive sprite adds 360 (the height of the screen) more to **ScrollY**.

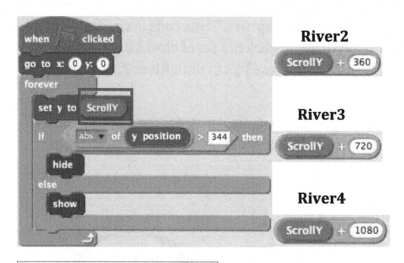

River2

ScrollY + 360

River3

ScrollY + 720

River4

ScrollY + 1080

> Click the **Green Flag** to test run this scene.

3. Animate the Moving Ground with Horizontal Scrolling

Go to Ch. 14 in our online resources, and open **Ground Horizontal Scroll – blank.sb2**. In this animation, **Ground1** and **Ground2** are the main scrolling sprites. When the **Cat** sprite moves to the left or right, the ground sprites scroll in the opposite direction.

For example, if the cat moves to the left, the ground sprites would scroll to the right.

When the second ground sprite reaches the edge of the screen,

This cycle repeats until you click the **Red Stop** sign. In order to program this technique, let's first create the variable **ScrollX** for all sprites.

Click the **Ground1** sprite and add:

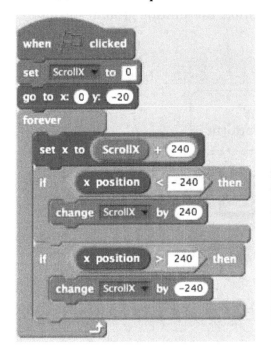

If **Ground1** is less than 240 (left part of screen), it shifts to the right.

If **Ground1** is greater than 240 (right part of screen), it shifts to the left.

Next, duplicate this script and drag-and-drop it over **Ground2**. Let'smake some minor changes to **Ground1's** script.

Replace the blocks boxed in red with the blocks on the right.

```
when [flag] clicked
set ScrollX to 0
go to x: 0 y: -20
forever
  set x to ( ScrollX + 240 )
  if < x position < -240 > then
    change ScrollX by 240
  if < x position > 240 > then
    change ScrollX by -240
```

go to x: 240 y: -20

set x to ScrollX

Ground2 appears on the screen. These new motion blocks keep **Ground2** side by side with **Ground1**.

95

Click the **Cat** sprite, and make it appear in motion by changing the **ScrollX** variable. Although the cat won't change position, the shifting ground sprites imply that it is moving.

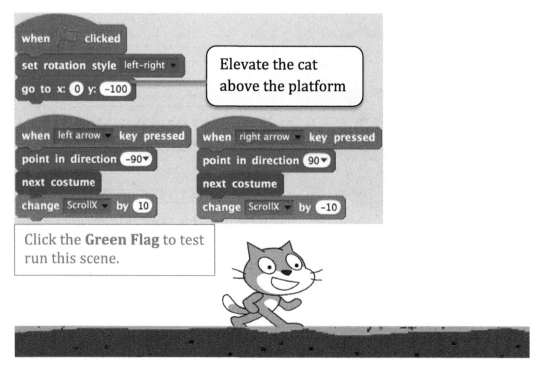

Elevate the cat above the platform

Click the **Green Flag** to test run this scene.

4. Animate the Background with Horizontal Scrolling

First, go to Ch. 14 in our online resources, and open **Background Vertical Scroll – Blank.sb2**. This Scratch project already contains the background and the **France** sprite. Click the **France** sprite and add:

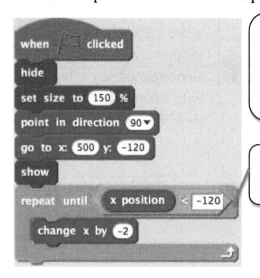

France already covers the screen from left to right. **Set Size to 150 %** makes it even bigger to create a zoomed-in effect.

France starts outside the screen and glides to the opposite end.

Click the **Green Flag** to test run this scene.

Chapter 15 - Snapshot Technique

In this chapter, we will animate a video clip of marine life, using snapshots. In the process, we will learn how to take snapshots of video clips and run them in Scratch so that it looks like a realistic motion picture.

1. Find a short 10-15 second video clip to use in your animation.

For our animation we will use the YouTube video, **Aquarium 2hr relax music,** by **milleaccendini**. Go onto your internet browser, and search this video clip in YouTube or go to
https://www.youtube.com/watch?v=VIrBecB746c .

If you cannot find this clip, don't worry. You can use any video clip is to learn how to take snapshots of video scenes. However, we will use snapshots from Ch. 15 in our online resources to build the animation.

2. Create a Snapshot Folder

Go inside the folder on your computer where you save your Scratch Projects, and create a new folder. Rename this folder **Snapshots**. You will place all of the snapshots you take in this folder.

Snapshots

3. Gather Snapshots

Starting from the beginning, play and pause your video at roughly half-second intervals. You must click the play/pause button incredibly fast, and watch for small change in the picture. While the video is paused, open your snapshot tool, and highlight the whole video. Take a snapshot of the video frame and save it to your newly created **Snapshots** folder.

Tips:
- Gather your snapshots in one sitting if possible. You can take short breaks if you feel tired.
- Avoid taking pictures with the media bar at the bottom of the video.
- Keep the width and height of your snapshots consistent. Otherwise, your animation may seem out of focus.

Here are some examples:

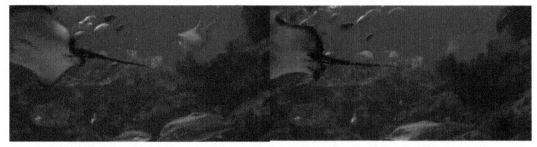

First Snapshot   **Second Snapshot**

Third Snapshot   **Fourth Snapshot**

Take at least five snapshots to become familiar with the process. **Make sure that you save them in order, whether alphabetically or numerically.** Collecting snapshots can be tedious. But don't worry. You can download the whole collection of snapshots from our online files.

4. Upload each Snapshot as a Costume

Create a project named **Snapshot Technique**, and delete the cat sprite. Next, click the folder icon 📤 to import a sprite from your computer. Choose the **Ocean.sprite2** in Ch. 15 of our online resources.

Caution: We saved you the trouble of adding snapshots. But when you do it yourself, add them as costumes one at a time. If you add them all at once, this may mess up the order of your snapshots and disrupt the flow of the overall animation.

5. Make the Ocean Come Alive

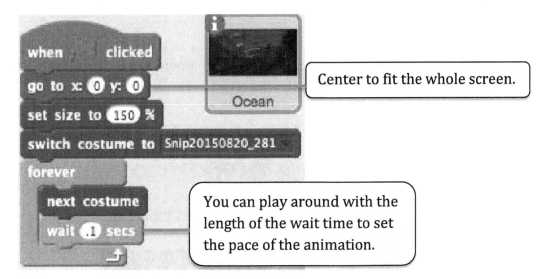

Center to fit the whole screen.

You can play around with the length of the wait time to set the pace of the animation.

Now go to the **Sound** tab, and click . Add the sound, **xylo1,** and program it into the animation.

xylo1

Click the **Green Flag** to test run this scene.

Chapter 16 - Oil in the Ocean Documentary

1. Create a Storyboard

In this chapter, we will create a project featuring the poem, **Oil in the Ocean**. Each line in the poem is animated and each scene is presented in a slideshow format.

Download the Scratch project template, **Oil in the Ocean – blank.sb2**, from Ch. 16 in our online resources. The template already contains every sprite along with their sounds and costumes. Let's first lay out the poem in our storyboard.

Scene 1	"The ocean is blue and I like it that way,"
Scene 2	"So please don't ruin it and turn it grey."
Scene 3	"The stinky smell of oil in the air, It's just too bad that people don't care."
Scene 4	"Wherever there's mucky, filthy oil,"
Scene 5	"The fish and birds struggle and toil."
Scene 6	"All the fish struggle and brood, but the ocean is in a silent mood."
Scene 7	"When the water is dirty and brown, I'm really down with a pale frown."
Scene 8	"I like the oil in the food that I eat, I just don't like crude in my crab meat."
Scene 9	"The cold ocean water is splashing at me, The oil is too, since it's been set free. If my poem has changed anything in you, I will be glad and the ocean will too."

Make sure to refer to your storyboard as we are programming. The poem itself is a sprite, and each scene is a costume. Other sprites compose each line's accompanying animation.

2. Program the First Scene

Go to the **Stage,** and create the **Storyboard Script**. Make sure to create a new broadcast, "**scene1**".

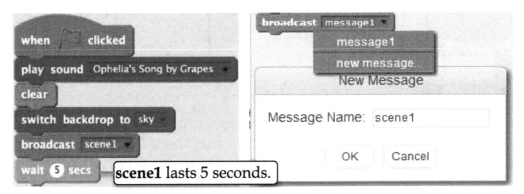

scene1 lasts 5 seconds.

Now let's simulate the waves of the ocean. Click the **Wave1** sprite.

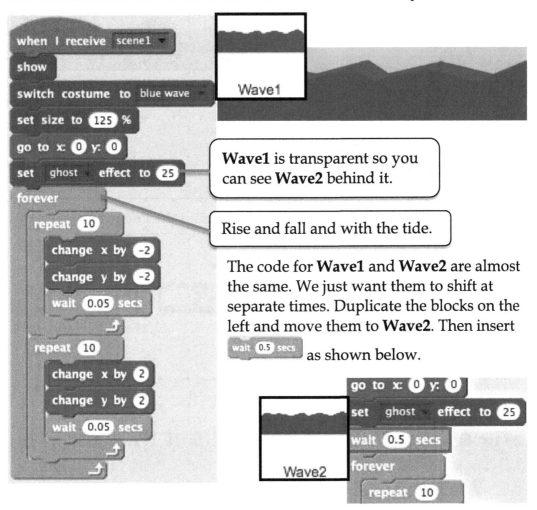

Wave1 is transparent so you can see **Wave2** behind it.

Rise and fall and with the tide.

The code for **Wave1** and **Wave2** are almost the same. We just want them to shift at separate times. Duplicate the blocks on the left and move them to **Wave2**. Then insert `wait 0.5 secs` as shown below.

Next let's make the first line of the poem appear while the waves are fluctuating. Add the blocks below to the **Poem** Sprite.

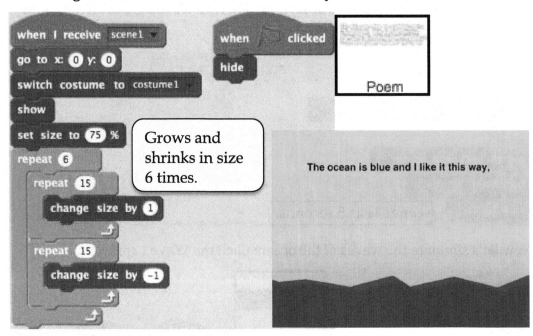

The last animated sprite for **scene1** that we have yet to program is the clouds. Go to the **Cloud** sprite.

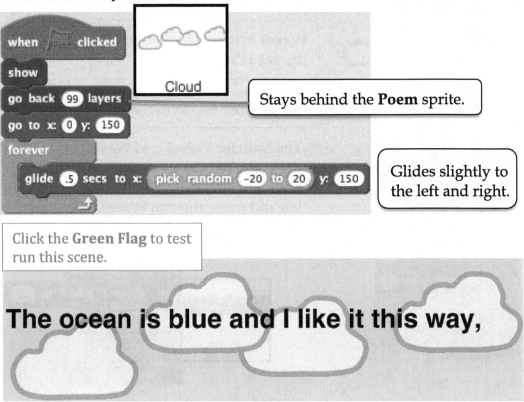

3. Program the Second Scene

 Go to the **Stage,** create a new broadcast, **scene2,** and add it to the **Storyboard Script**.

Go to the **Poem** sprite to change its costume to the next line in Oil in the Ocean.

Next, let's turn **Wave1** and **Wave2** to the color, gray.

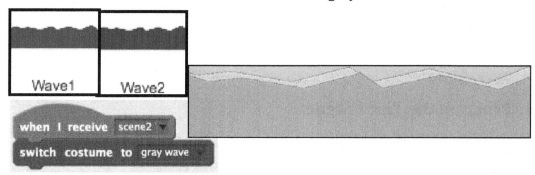

The main animation in **scene2** is the simulation of grey raindrops. Go to the **Rain** sprite, and add the blocks below. Notice this sprite has no visible costume. It just uses **Pen**.

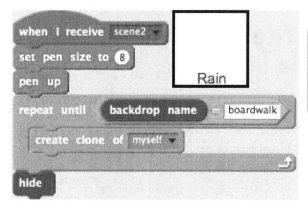

Next, let's program each clone to mimic a grey raindrop.

backdrop name can be found in **Looks. boardwalk** is **scene3**'s backdrop. Here it will rain until we switch the backdrop to **boardwalk.**

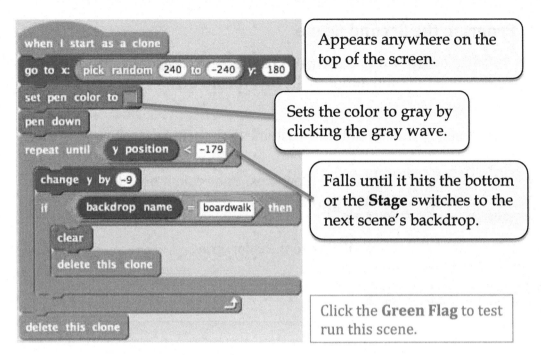

when I start as a clone	Appears anywhere on the top of the screen.
go to x: pick random 240 to -240 y: 180	
set pen color to ▢	Sets the color to gray by clicking the gray wave.
pen down	
repeat until y position < -179	Falls until it hits the bottom or the **Stage** switches to the next scene's backdrop.
change y by -9	
if backdrop name = boardwalk then	
clear	
delete this clone	
delete this clone	Click the **Green Flag** to test run this scene.

4. Program the Third Scene

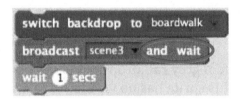

Go to the **Stage,** and add **scene3** to the **Storyboard Script.** Make sure this **Broadcast** block ends with **and wait**.

Click the **Poem** sprite to change its costume to the next line in the poem.

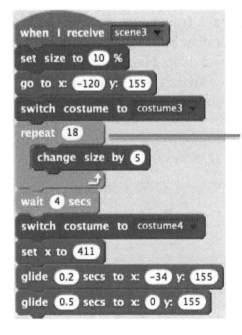

The stinky smell of is in the air.

Uses the Word Technique – Zoom in.

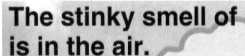

It's just too bad that people don't care

Uses the Word Technique – Slide in.

104

Poem's **costume3** doesn't seem right. That's because it's missing the word, oil! Let's animate each of the letters in this word.

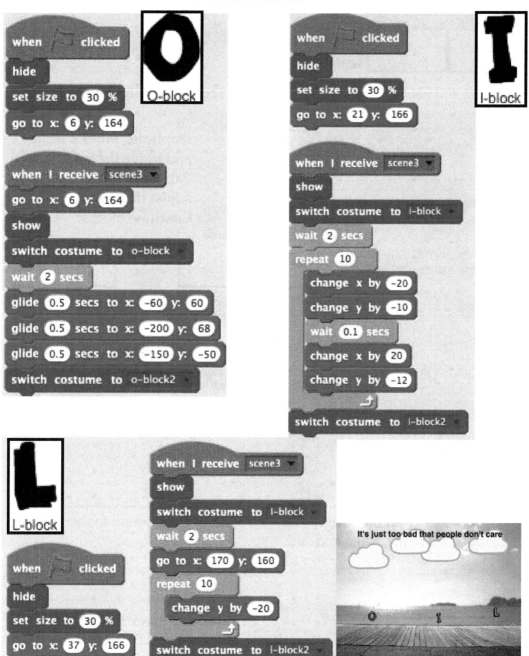

Almost forget about our wave sprites? We need to hide them during **scene3**.

Next, let's add wind to this scene through the **Tree1** and **Palmtree** sprites.

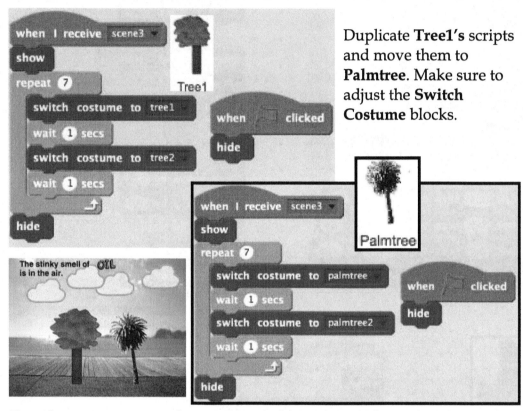

Duplicate **Tree1's** scripts and move them to **Palmtree**. Make sure to adjust the **Switch Costume** blocks.

Now that we programmed scenes 1,2, and 3, we can add sound to the animations. Go to the **Stage** and add:

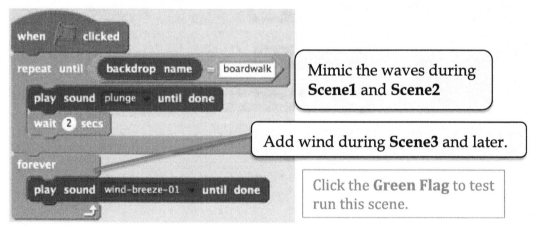

Mimic the waves during **Scene1** and **Scene2**

Add wind during **Scene3** and later.

Click the **Green Flag** to test run this scene.

5. Program the Fourth Scene

 In the **Stage,** also add **scene4** to the **Storyboard Script.**

Remember that the **O-block, I-block**, and **L-block** are still showing from the previous scene? Now it's time to hide them.

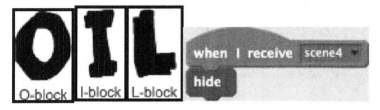

Go to the **Poem** sprite to change its costume to the next line in Oil in the Ocean.

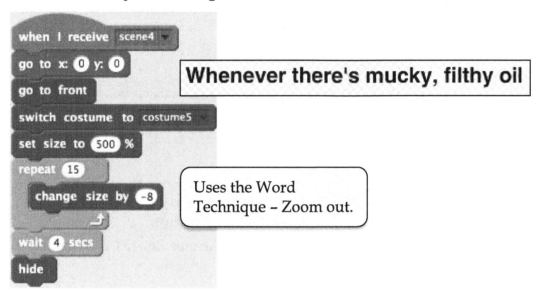

Whenever there's mucky, filthy oil

Uses the Word Technique – Zoom out.

This and future scenes are no longer suitable for the **Cloud** sprite. So let's hide the clouds.

Next, go to the **Ocean** sprite. This sprite takes up the whole screen. In this scene, **Ocean** cycles through its costumes of the oil polluted waters.

1	2	3	4	5
Ocean Oil	Ocean Oil 2	Ocean Oil 3	Ocean Oil 4	Ocean Oil 5

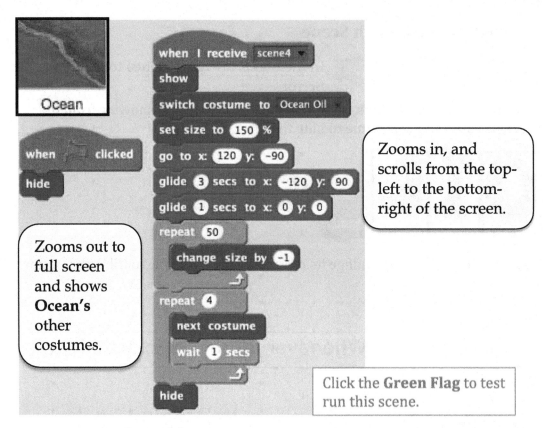

Ocean

when [flag] clicked
hide

when I receive scene4
show
switch costume to Ocean Oil
set size to 150 %
go to x: 120 y: -90
glide 3 secs to x: -120 y: 90
glide 1 secs to x: 0 y: 0
repeat 50
  change size by -1
repeat 4
  next costume
  wait 1 secs
hide

Zooms in, and scrolls from the top-left to the bottom-right of the screen.

Zooms out to full screen and shows **Ocean's** other costumes.

Click the **Green Flag** to test run this scene.

6. Program the Fifth Scene

broadcast scene5 and wait

Go to the **Stage** and add **scene5** to the **Storyboard Script**.

Go to the **Poem** sprite to change its costume to the next line in Oil in the Ocean.

when I receive scene5
go to x: 0 y: 160
switch costume to costume6
show

The fish and birds struggle and toil.

Now let's show pictures of fish and birds struggling in the oil.

Fish and Bird.. Fish and Bird.. Fish and Bird...Fish and Bird...Fish and Bird... Fish and Bird...

108

Go to the **Fish and Birds** sprite. Cycle through each costume using all of the graphic effects except color.

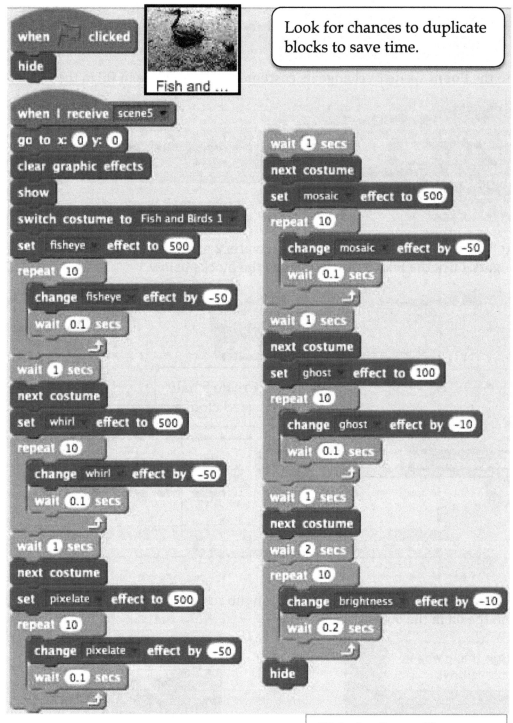

when ⚑ clicked
hide

Fish and ...

Look for chances to duplicate blocks to save time.

when I receive scene5
go to x: 0 y: 0
clear graphic effects
show
switch costume to Fish and Birds 1
set fisheye effect to 500
repeat 10
    change fisheye effect by -50
    wait 0.1 secs
wait 1 secs
next costume
set whirl effect to 500
repeat 10
    change whirl effect by -50
    wait 0.1 secs
wait 1 secs
next costume
set pixelate effect to 500
repeat 10
    change pixelate effect by -50
    wait 0.1 secs

wait 1 secs
next costume
set mosaic effect to 500
repeat 10
    change mosaic effect by -50
    wait 0.1 secs
wait 1 secs
next costume
set ghost effect to 100
repeat 10
    change ghost effect by -10
    wait 0.1 secs
wait 1 secs
next costume
wait 2 secs
repeat 10
    change brightness effect by -10
    wait 0.2 secs
hide

Combine the two large sets of block above.

Click the **Green Flag** to test run this scene.

7. Program the Sixth Scene

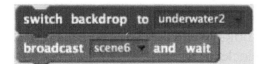

Go to the **Stage** and add **scene6** to the **Storyboard Script**.

Go to the **Poem** sprite to change its costume to the next line in Oil in the Ocean.

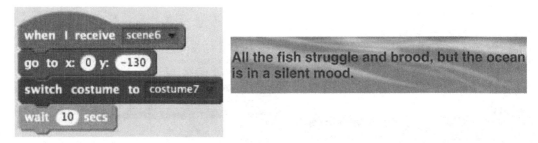

All the fish struggle and brood, but the ocean is in a silent mood.

Next, let's switch the backdrop to **underwater2** and observe the fish's thoughts. Click the **Fish2** sprite, and add the blocks below.

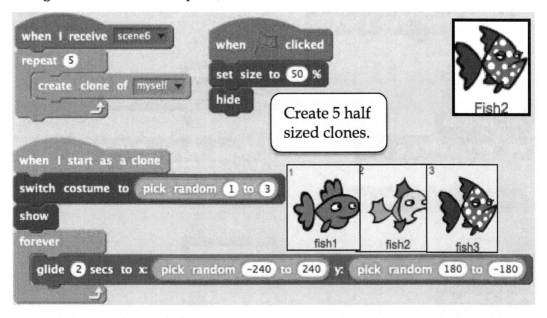

Create 5 half sized clones.

Aside from gliding to random locations on the screen, the fish also complain about the oil in the ocean.

Ugh this place is filthy!

This oil stinks!

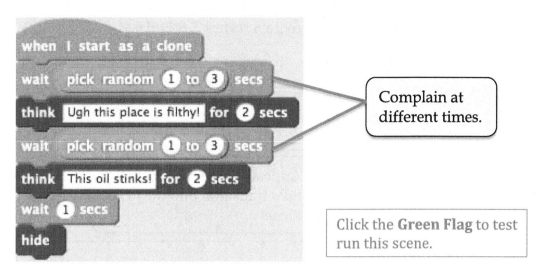

Complain at different times.

Click the **Green Flag** to test run this scene.

8. Program the Seventh, Eighth, and Ninth Scene

Go to the **Stage** to program the final scenes of the **Storyboard Script**. We grouped them together because they only animate the words (**Poem** sprite) of the Oil in the Ocean poem.

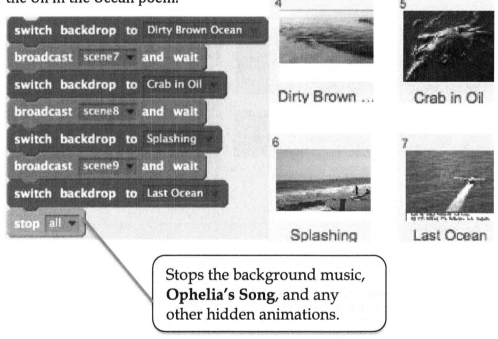

Dirty Brown ...

Crab in Oil

Splashing

Last Ocean

Stops the background music, **Ophelia's Song,** and any other hidden animations.

Now let's go to the **Poem** Sprite to program scenes 7, 8, and 9.

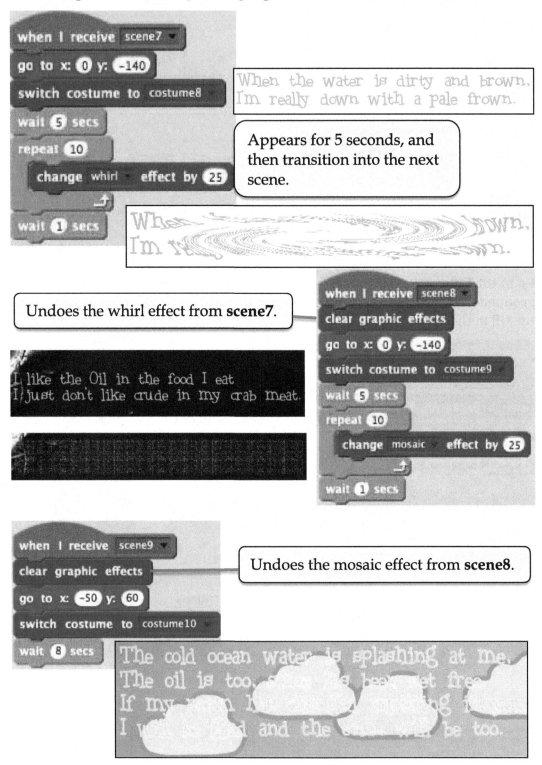

Now click the **Green Flag,** and enjoy your animated poem!

Chapter 17 - The Robositter Movie Trailer

1. Create a Storyboard

In this chapter, we will create a movie trailer animation featuring the relationship between Lucas and Robositter, his robot babysitter.

First, let's choose our main sprites.

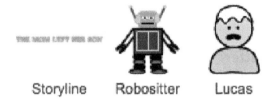

Storyline   Robositter   Lucas

Second, let's choose our secondary sprites. These sprites are only used occasionally in the animation, and they keep the story moving.

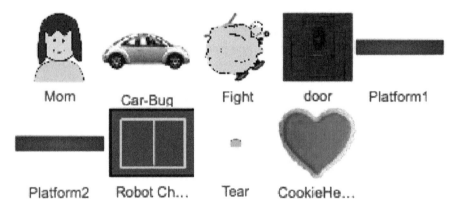

Mom   Car-Bug   Fight   door   Platform1

Platform2   Robot Ch...   Tear   CookieHe...

Download the Scratch project template, **The Robositter – blank.sb2** from Ch. 17 in our online resources. The movie trailer will have alternating text scenes and animations. Let's outline each scene in our storyboard.

Storyline	Animation
1. THE MOM LEFT HER SON	**Mom:** Says "By son, I'm going to Japan." Drives to Japan from left to right.
2. WITH A ROBOT BABYSITTER	**Robositter:** Whirls into view. Says "Hello, I'm your new robositter." **Lucas:** Shows distressed face. Zoom in on eyes which become bloodshot.

3. FEATURING SPECTACULAR ACTION	**Lucas:** Shows distressed face. Disappears in a cloud of smoke. Runs away with fists raised. **Robositter:** "Come back and brush your teeth." Appears in front of Lucas. **Lucas/Robositter:** Both collide, and have a fight.
4. AND A HEARTWARMING FRIENDSHIP	**Lucas:** Gives Robositter heart. **Robositter:** Starts crying with happiness. Puts heart into chest. Heart starts beating inside him.
5. CRITICS ARE AMAZED	
6. THE ROBOSITTER	
7. COMING SOON THIS FALL	

Make sure to refer to the storyboard as we are programming.

2. Program the First Scene

Click the **Stage** and create the **Storyboard Script**. When adding broadcast blocks, make sure they have **and wait** at the end.

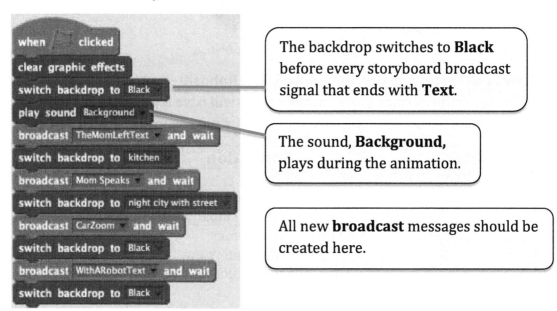

The backdrop switches to **Black** before every storyboard broadcast signal that ends with **Text**.

The sound, **Background,** plays during the animation.

All new **broadcast** messages should be created here.

Now let's program the **Storyline** sprite.

Centers the storyline to prevent any positioning errors.

Go to the **More Blocks** section, and click Make a Block . Name the block "**Next Scene**". Pull up the drop-down menu, and add a number input next to the purple block, **Next Scene,** and name it "**costume#**".

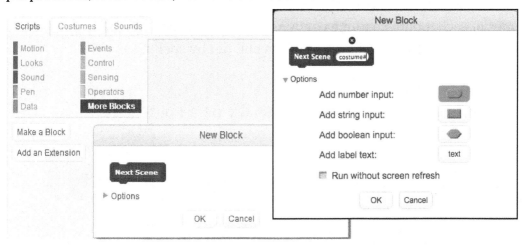

Let's program this procedure to change to transition into scenes by fading in and out.

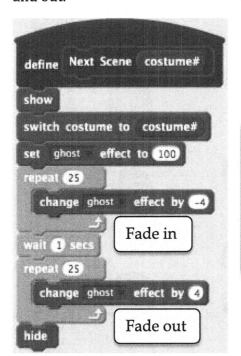

Fade in

Fade out

This set of blocks is run by Next Scene ❶ . In computer science, we call it **procedure** or **function**. Instead of typing this block of code many times, we simply use one block Next Scene ❶ . This makes the code more readable and easier to maintain.

Now let's use this **Procedure** to show the first costume of the **Storyline** sprite.

`when I receive TheMomLeftText`
`Next Scene 1` THE MOM LEFT HER SON

Next, we have to program **Mom Left Her Son** in scene1. Click the **Mom** sprite, and add the blocks below. She is supposed to lip sync with the sound recording, **Mom Talking**. Each costume represents a different sound. The names of each mouth costume contains the sounds that they represent. The costumes are ordered by sounding them out, not by spelling.

Mom: "Bye son, I'm going to Japan."

Costume Translation: B-I S-O-N I-M G-O-E-G T-O J-A-P-A-N

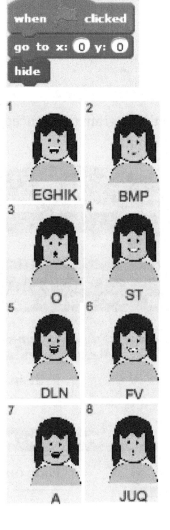

116

Combine these two long sets of blocks to sound out the full sentence. Make sure to test it by clicking the block.

Next, let's program the **Car Sprite**. In this scene, Lucas's mother drives to Japan. Click the **Car-Bug** sprite, and add the blocks below.

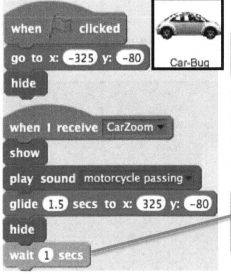

The car starts on the left side of the screen and glides towards the right side.

Gives the audience time to register what happens and prevents the animation from moving too quickly.

Click the **Green Flag** to test run this scene.

3. Program the Second Scene

Click the **Stage,** and add these blocks to the **Storyboard Script.** Keep in mind that the blocks end with **and wait**.

Next, click the **Storyline** sprite and program the next piece of text in the trailer.

This time, the **Next Scene** block switches to **Storyline's** second costume. Let's program **door** sprite to open.

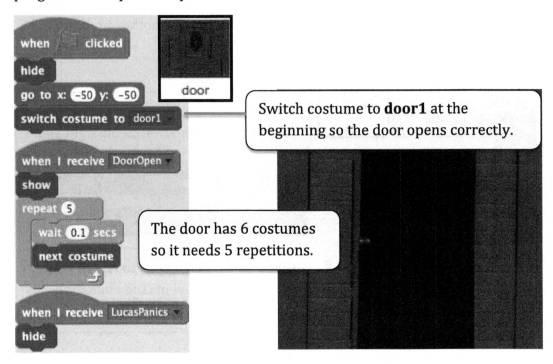

Switch costume to **door1** at the beginning so the door opens correctly.

The door has 6 costumes so it needs 5 repetitions.

Next, let's program the **Robositter** sprite to appear in front of the door.

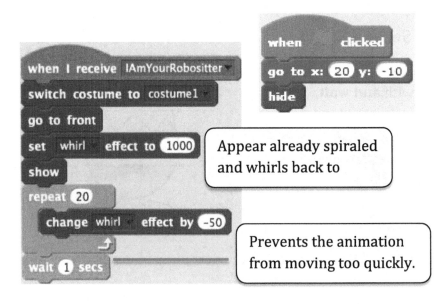

Appear already spiraled and whirls back to

Prevents the animation from moving too quickly.

Beneath this script, add the blocks in the figure below.

These blocks program the Robositter to say, *"Hello, I'm your new robositter."*

The number of repetitions is set to end when the sound, **IAmYourRobositter**, ends.

Now let's program the **Lucas** sprite to panic when he sees **Robositter**.

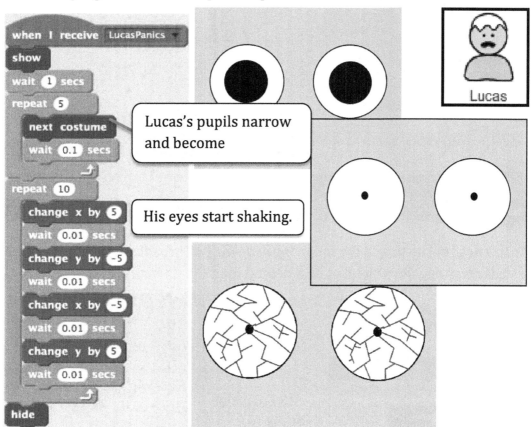

Lucas's pupils narrow and become

His eyes start shaking.

Don't forget to set Lucas's starting properties.

Click the **Green Flag** to test run this scene.

4. Program the Third Scene

Click the **Stage,** and add these blocks to the **Storyboard Script**.

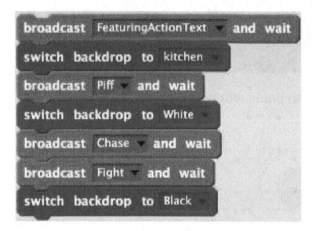

Click the **Storytelling** sprite and add:

Go to **Lucas** sprite to add the following code for **Piff** broadcast. In this scene, he speeds away leaving a cloud of dust behind him.

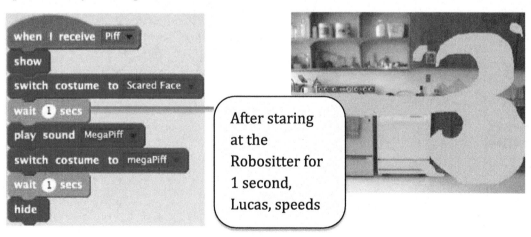

After staring at the Robositter for 1 second, Lucas, speeds

Next, Lucas runs away from his Robositter. The Robositter then suddenly appears in front of him. They collide, triggering the fight.

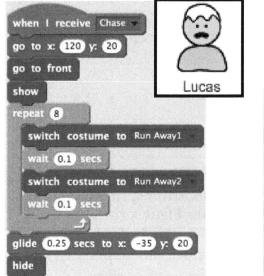

Lucas

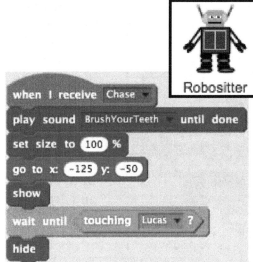

Robositter

Let's program Lucas's running on the two platforms sprites.

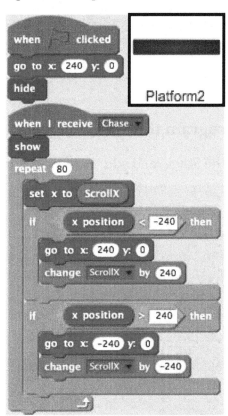

Platform1   **Platform2**

121

Both platforms move to the right while Lucas is running. Lucas and both moving platforms are timed to stop at the same time.

Go to the **Fight** sprite and animate it.

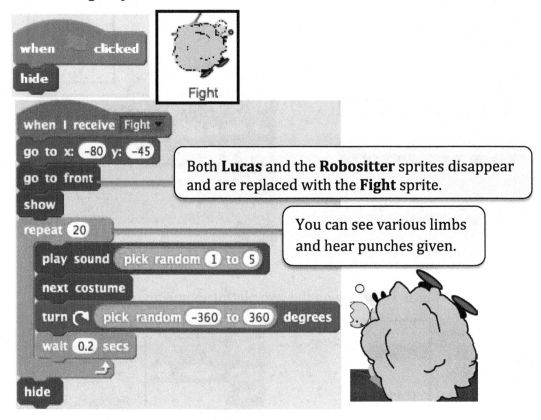

Fight

when clicked
hide

when I receive Fight
go to x: -80 y: -45
go to front
show
repeat 20
    play sound pick random 1 to 5
    next costume
    turn ↻ pick random -360 to 360 degrees
    wait 0.2 secs
hide

Both **Lucas** and the **Robositter** sprites disappear and are replaced with the **Fight** sprite.

You can see various limbs and hear punches given.

5. Program the Fourth Scene

Click the **Stage,** and add these blocks to the **Storyboard Script.**

broadcast AndaHeartWarmingText and wait
switch backdrop to kitchen
broadcast GiveHeart and wait
broadcast RobotTears and wait
broadcast CloseChest and wait
broadcast Heartbeat and wait
switch backdrop to Black
broadcast Critics and wait
broadcast TheRobositterText and wait
broadcast ComingSoonText and wait
stop all sounds

122

When the fight ends, make sure **Platform1** and **Platform2** disappear.

Click the **Green Flag** to test run this scene.

Go to the **Storytelling** sprite and add:

Now let's program the **Cookieheart** sprite with **GiveHeart** broadcast. In this scene, **Lucas** gives a baked heart to his **Robositter**.

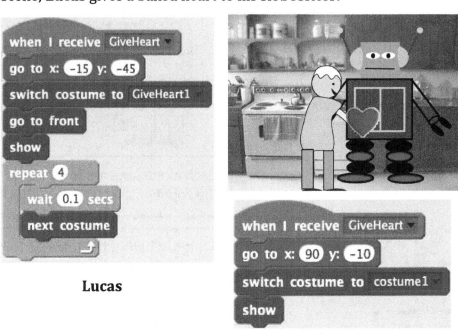

Lucas

Robositter

The **Robositter** starts crying with happiness when **RobotTears** broadcast. First, go to the **Robositter** sprite and add:

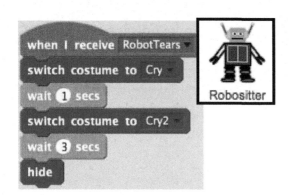

```
when I receive RobotTears
switch costume to Cry
wait 1 secs
switch costume to Cry2
wait 3 secs
hide
```

Robositter

Then, click on Lucas and time when he hides.

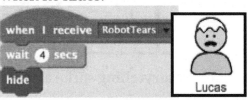

```
when I receive RobotTears
wait 4 secs
hide
```

Lucas

Let's program **Tear** sprite. Make the **Robositter's** tears fall to the ground.

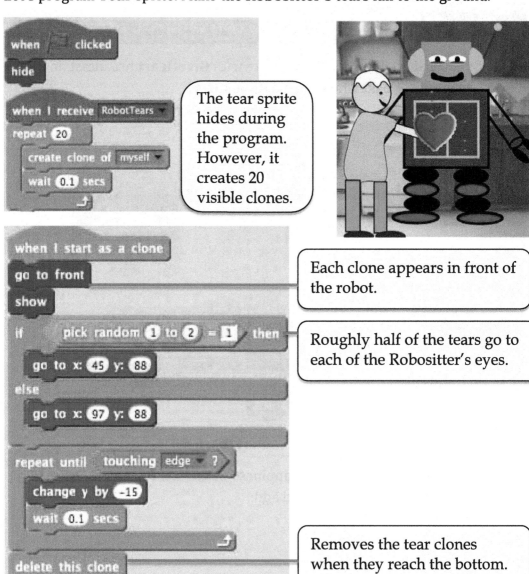

```
when [flag] clicked
hide
```

```
when I receive RobotTears
repeat 20
    create clone of myself
    wait 0.1 secs
```

> The tear sprite hides during the program. However, it creates 20 visible clones.

```
when I start as a clone
go to front
show
if  pick random 1 to 2 = 1  then
    go to x: 45 y: 88
else
    go to x: 97 y: 88

repeat until  touching edge ?
    change y by -15
    wait 0.1 secs

delete this clone
```

> Each clone appears in front of the robot.

> Roughly half of the tears go to each of the Robositter's eyes.

> Removes the tear clones when they reach the bottom.

124

Next, let's zoom into the **Robositter's** chest and watch it close around the heart. Go to the **Robot Chest** sprite and drag the blocks below:

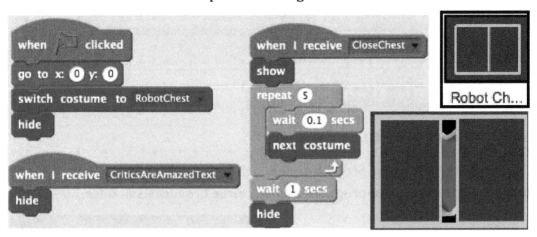

Now let's program **CookieHeart** sprite. The **Heartbeat** broadcast shows the Robositter's heart beating inside his chest. Go to the **CookieHeart** sprite.

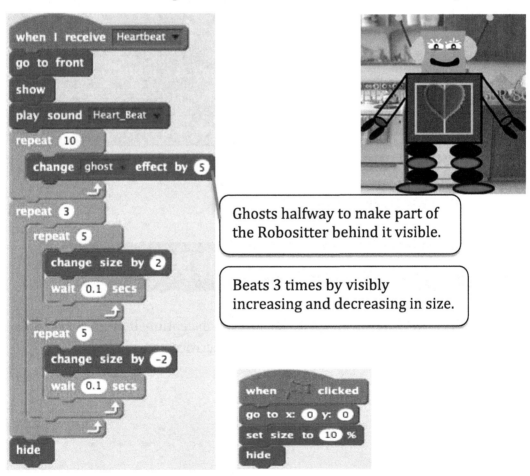

Ghosts halfway to make part of the Robositter behind it visible.

Beats 3 times by visibly increasing and decreasing in size.

Go to the **Robositter** sprite, and add the blocks below:

Click the **Green Flag** to test run this scene.

6. Program the Fifth Scene

These blocks just display **Storyline** slides in front of a **Black** background. Go to the **Storyline** sprite, and program the next three broadcasts at once.

However, the **Storyline** sprites' **fifth** scene is an exception. It must stay visible longer so that the audience has time to read the critics' comments.

Go to the script starting with 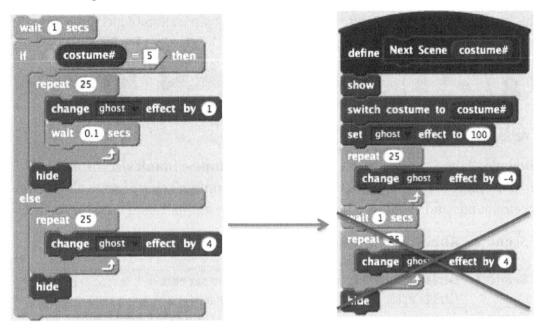. Delete the second repeat block and replace it with the blocks below:

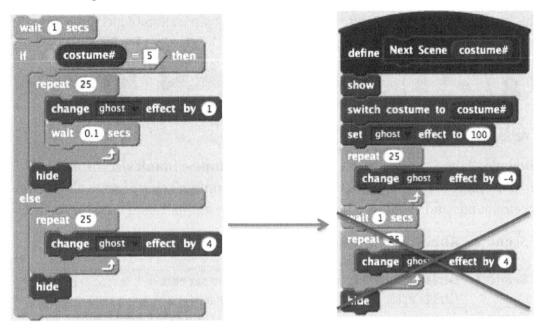

Now click the **Green Flag** to run your awesome Movie Trailer Animation!

Chapter 18 - The Jump Rope Challenge

1. Create a Storyboard

In this chapter, we will create a project featuring a passionate girl jump roper who practices regardless of other distractions.

Abbey Girl1 Girl2 Cloud Sun Moon Girl3 Hot Air Ba... Poem

Download the Scratch project template, **Jump Rope – blank.sb2**, from Ch. 18 in our online resources. This template already contains every sprite along with their sounds and costumes. Let's first lay out the animation in our storyboard.

Scene 1	**Abbey**: Starts jump roping. **Cloud**: Appears in the sky.
Scene 2	**Girl1 and Girl2**: Jump ropes onto the screen. **Girl1**: asks, *"Want to do something else?"*
Scene 3	**Abbey**: Stops jump roping, says, *"No thank you. I need more practice!"* and resumes jump roping. **Sun**: Arcs across the screen, indicating that time is passing.
Scene 4	**Girl1** and **Girl2**: Jump ropes off the screen. **Stage**: Darkens slightly.
Scene 5	**Girl3**: Asks, *"Want a snack?"* **Abbey**: Stops, says, *"No thank you. I need more practice!"*, and resumes jump roping.
Scene 6	**Stage**: Darkens slightly. **Hot Air Balloon**: Says, *"Abbey! Come ride with us!"* **Abbey**: Stops jump roping, says, *"No thank you. I need more practice!"* and resumes jump roping.
Scene 7	**Cloud**: Disappears from screen. **Stage**: Darkens considerably. **Moon**: Arcs across the screen, indicating that time is passing. **Poem**: Scrolls across screen, like credits in a movie.
Scene 8	**Abbey**: Stops jump roping, and falls asleep. **Abbey and Stage**: Darkens until black.

Make sure to refer to your storyboard as we are programming.

2. Program the First Scene

Go to the **Stage,** and create four variables: **Abbey Done, Girl1 Done, Girl2 Done**, and **Clouds Done** for all sprites. Then add the blocks below to the **Storyboard Script**.

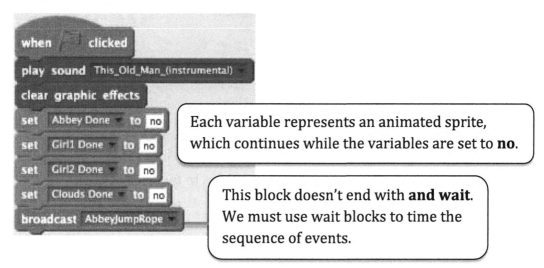

Each variable represents an animated sprite, which continues while the variables are set to **no**.

This block doesn't end with **and wait**. We must use wait blocks to time the sequence of events.

Click the **Abbey** sprite. Let's program the **AbbeyJumpRope** broadcast to start Abbey jump roping.

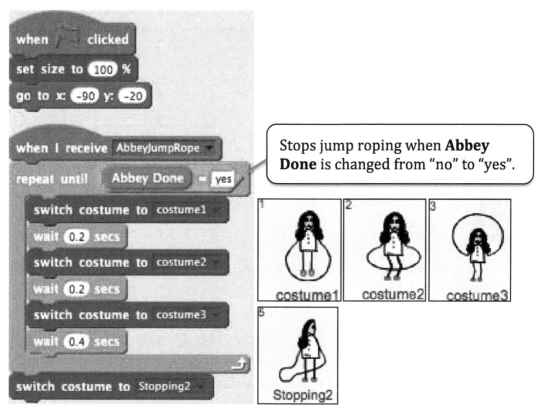

Stops jump roping when **Abbey Done** is changed from "no" to "yes".

129

Next, click the **Cloud** sprite. In order to make it appear at the beginning of the program, we have to create the procedures, **fade in** and **fade out**.

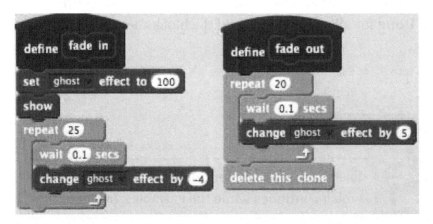

Now let's produce cloud clones, and program them to fade in and out.

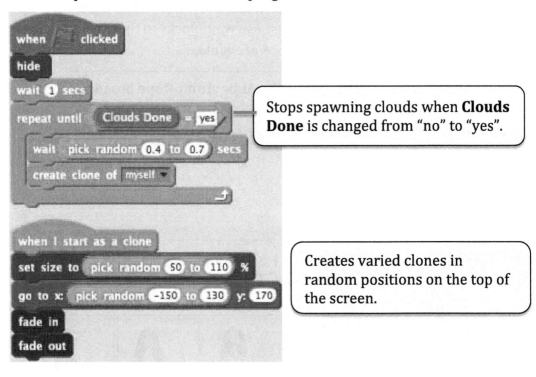

Stops spawning clouds when **Clouds Done** is changed from "no" to "yes".

Creates varied clones in random positions on the top of the screen.

Click the **Green Flag** to test run this scene.

3. Program the Second Scene

Click the **Stage,** and drag the blocks below.

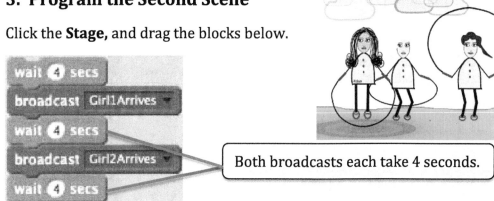

```
wait 4 secs
broadcast Girl1Arrives
wait 4 secs
broadcast Girl2Arrives
wait 4 secs
```

> Both broadcasts each take 4 seconds.

Now let's go to **Girl1** and program her interaction with **Abbey**.

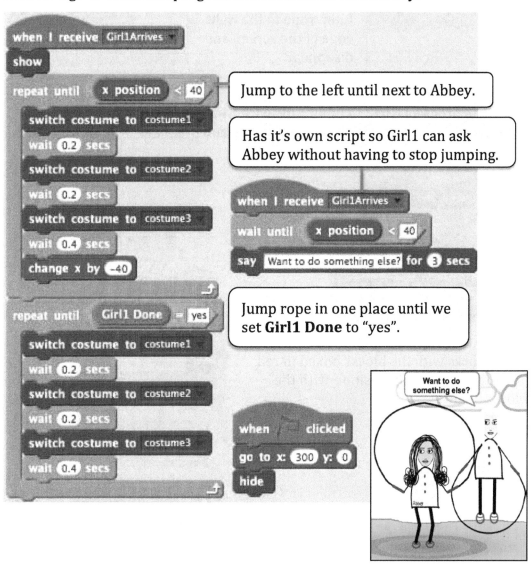

```
when I receive Girl1Arrives
show
repeat until  x position < 40
    switch costume to costume1
    wait 0.2 secs
    switch costume to costume2
    wait 0.2 secs
    switch costume to costume3
    wait 0.4 secs
    change x by -40
repeat until  Girl1 Done = yes
    switch costume to costume1
    wait 0.2 secs
    switch costume to costume2
    wait 0.2 secs
    switch costume to costume3
    wait 0.4 secs
```

> Jump to the left until next to Abbey.

> Has it's own script so Girl1 can ask Abbey without having to stop jumping.

```
when I receive Girl1Arrives
wait until  x position < 40
say Want to do something else? for 3 secs
```

> Jump rope in one place until we set **Girl1 Done** to "yes".

```
when [flag] clicked
go to x: 300 y: 0
hide
```

131

Next, let's program **Girl1** leaving Abbey after **Girl Done** = "yes".

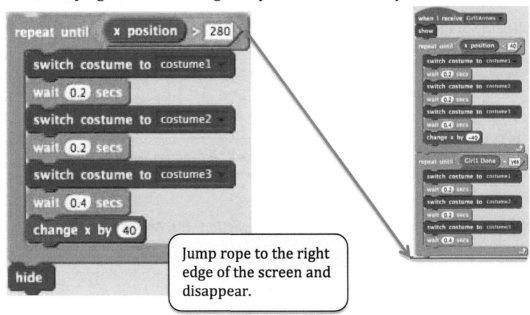

Jump rope to the right edge of the screen and disappear.

Next, let's program **Girl2** to jump rope with **Girl1**. **Girl2** just has to stop in a different place. Duplicate **Girl1's** giant script, and drag-and-drop it over **Girl2**.

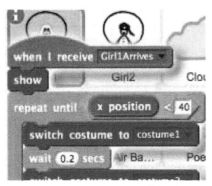

Replace the parts of the **Girl2's** **Repeat Until** blocks with the blocks boxed in red. Then set her starting position with the blocks below:

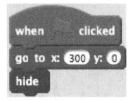

Click the **Green Flag** to test run this scene.

4. Program the Third Scene

Click the **Stage,** and add these blocks to the **Storyboard Script**.

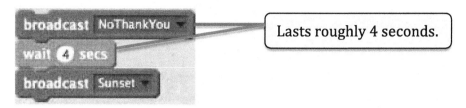

Lasts roughly 4 seconds.

```
broadcast NoThankYou
wait 4 secs
broadcast Sunset
```

Now let's program the **NoThankYou** broadcast. Click the **Abbey** sprite.

```
when I receive NoThankYou
set Abbey Done to yes
wait 0.5 secs
switch costume to Stopping1
wait 0.1 secs
switch costume to Stopping2
say No thank you. I need more practice! for 3 secs
wait 1 secs
set Abbey Done to no
broadcast AbbeyJumpRope
```

Abbey stops jump roping.

Stopping1   Stopping2

Abbey resumes jump roping.

No thank you. I need more practice!

After Abbey declines **Girl1**'s proposal, she continues to jump rope for a while. **Sunset** is broadcasted to signify the time passing quickly. Click the **Sun** sprite.

when I receive Sunset ▾
show
set size to 40 %
go to x: 210 y: -80
set x speed ▾ to -13
set y speed ▾ to 25

> Sets the initial trajectory to the upper and to the left.

repeat until touching edge ▾ ?
  go back 1 layers
  change x by x speed
  change y by y speed
  change y speed ▾ by -1.5
  wait 0.3 secs

> Passes behind the clouds and jump ropes.

> Simulates gravity. It moves just like the basketball in Ch. 6's **Basketball Toss.sb2**.

hide

when 🏳 clicked
hide
go to x: 0 y: 250

Click the **Green Flag** to test run this scene.

134

5. Program the Fourth Scene

Click the **Stage.** It is supposed to darken slightly in this scene. However, we also darken the **Stage** later in the Storyboard Script so let's create the procedure, **Darken number1 times.** This saves you time and space.

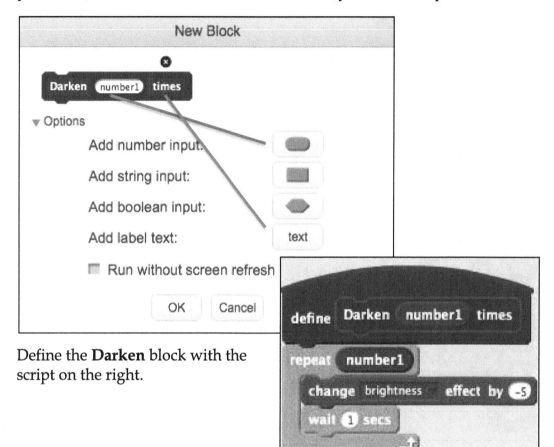

Define the **Darken** block with the script on the right.

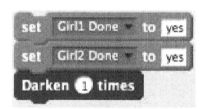

Both girl sprites start jumping towards the edge of the screen.

In this scene, the Stage darkens, and the other girls leave Abbey to her practice.

Click the **Green Flag** to test run this scene.

6. Program the Fifth Scene

Click the **Stage,** and add these blocks to the **Storyboard Script.**

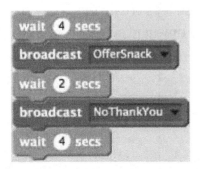

We already programmed the **NoThankYou** broadcast, but we still need to go to **Girl3,** and program the **OfferSnack** broadcast.

7. Program the Sixth Scene

Click the **Stage,** and add these blocks to the **Storyboard Script**.

Now let's go to the **Hot Air Balloon** sprite and program **OfferRide**. In this broadcast, the girls in the hot air balloon offer Abbey a ride while the balloon floats across the screen.

When you run the program, Abbey looks huge in comparison with the hot air balloon. Let's go to the **Abbey** sprite, and make it smaller.

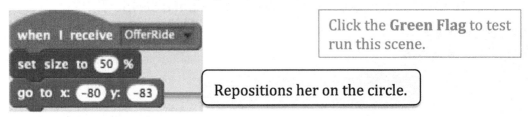

Click the **Green Flag** to test run this scene.

Repositions her on the circle.

8. Program the Seventh Scene

Click the **Stage,** and add these blocks to the **Storyboard Script.**

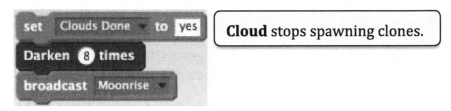

Cloud stops spawning clones.

Now let's program the **Moon** sprite. In the **Moonrise** broadcast, the moon arcs across the screen like the **Sun** sprite. Let's just duplicate all of the **Sun's** blocks into **Moon's** script. Make sure to adjust the values boxed in red.

During **Moonrise**, the **Poem** sprite scrolls vertically across the screen.

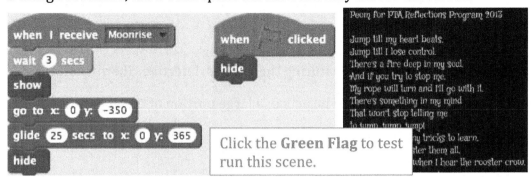

9. Program the Eighth Scene

Go to the **Stage,** and add these blocks to the **Storyboard Script.**

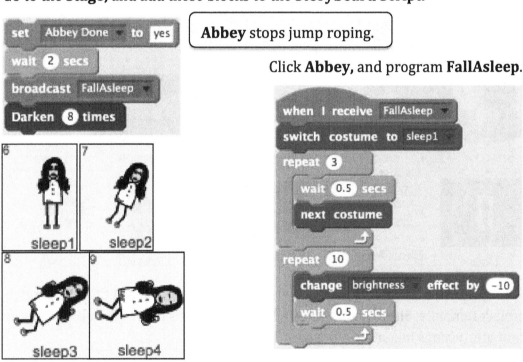

Now click the **Green Flag**, and enjoy your animation!

Chapter 19 - Sherlock Holmes' Adventure

1. Create a Storyboard

We will create an animation featuring the famous detective, Sherlock Holmes.

He is the only main sprite, and he acts in a large portion of the animation.

Sherlock

We also have a large collection of secondary sprites. These sprites interact with each other and the **Sherlock** sprite. But as small pieces of the project, they each will only appear in one scene.

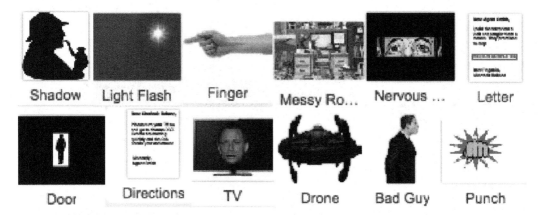

Download each sprite along with their sounds and costumes in Ch. 19's Scratch project template, **Sherlock Holmes – blank.sb2**. Let's first lay out the series of animated scenes in our storyboard.

Scene 1	A window opens and slowly reveals the **Shadow** of Sherlock Holmes. **Light Flash** will fade in and out. **Door** opens showing the Sherlock in the dark.
Scene 2	Sherlock's **Finger** turns on the lights. Sherlock scans the **Messy Room** and discovers a letter. Zoom in on **Nervous Eyes**, which starts shaking.
Scene 3	**Directions** scrolls from the bottom of the screen to the top, and tells Sherlock to turn on the TV.

	Agent Smith on the **TV** gives Sherlock his mission.
Scene 4	**Sherlock** flies on the drone and enters the Laboratory.
Scene 5	**Sherlock** rushes at the **Bad Guy**
	Punch appears as Sherlock fights the Bad Guy.
Scene 6	**Sherlock** leaves the Laboratory on his **Drone**.
	A **Letter** from Sherlock to Agent Smith scrolls from the bottom to the top saying "*Mission Completed*".

Make sure to refer to your storyboard as we are programming.

2. Program the First Scene

Click the **Stage,** and create the **Storyboard Script**.

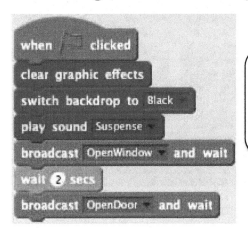

Keep in mind whether the **Looks** and **Event** blocks end with **and wait**. Using the wrong block can mess up the animation's sequence of events.

Now let's program the **OpenWindow** broadcast event to slowly unveil Sherlock.

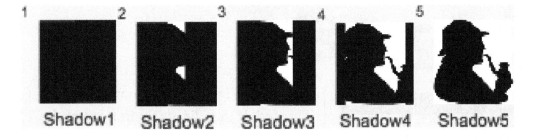

Shadow1   Shadow2   Shadow3   Shadow4   Shadow5

Click the **Shadow** sprite. Let's program it to open the window, flash a lighting effect, and pixelate out of view.

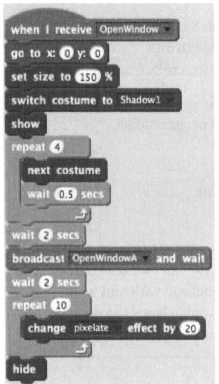

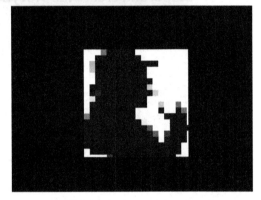

Now program the broadcast, **OpenWindowA**, to produce a lighting effect for our **Shadow** sprite. Click the **Light Flash** sprite and add:

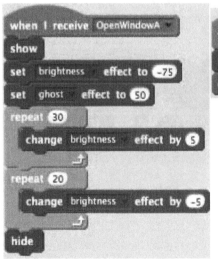

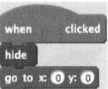

The **Light Flash** starts as darkened and ghosted. It then lights up in front of the **Shadow** sprite and darkens again.

Next, click the **Door** sprite, and show Sherlock opening the door to a dark room.

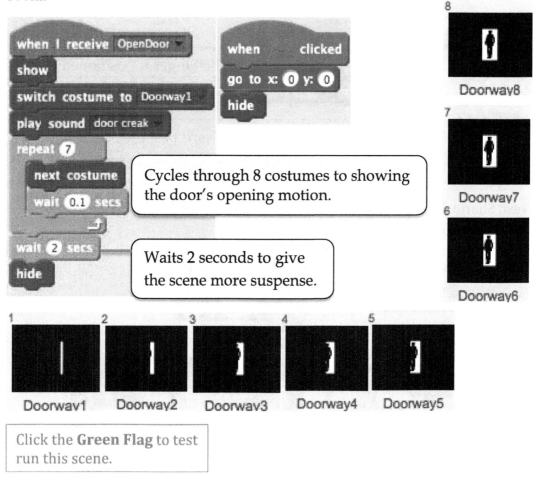

```
when I receive OpenDoor
show
switch costume to Doorway1
play sound door creak
repeat 7
    next costume
    wait 0.1 secs
wait 2 secs
hide
```

```
when   clicked
go to x: 0 y: 0
hide
```

Cycles through 8 costumes to showing the door's opening motion.

Waits 2 seconds to give the scene more suspense.

8

Doorway8

7

Doorway7

6

Doorway6

1   2   3   4   5

Doorway1   Doorway2   Doorway3   Doorway4   Doorway5

Click the **Green Flag** to test run this scene.

3. Program the Second Scene

Click the **Stage,** and drag the blocks below to the **Storyboard Script**.

```
switch backdrop to Light Switch
broadcast LightsOn and wait
broadcast ScanRoom and wait
play sound Discovery
broadcast NervousEyes and wait
```

Now let's go program the **Finger** sprite with the **LightsOn** broadcast. In this broadcast, Sherlock turns on the lights, and withdraws his hand.

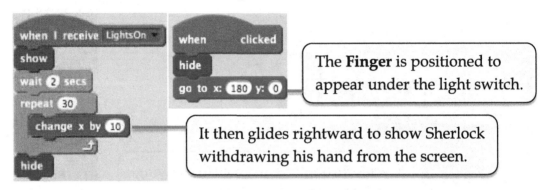

The **Finger** is positioned to appear under the light switch.

It then glides rightward to show Sherlock withdrawing his hand from the screen.

Next, Sherlock receives the broadcast, **ScanRoom**. Go to the **Messy Room** sprite and add:

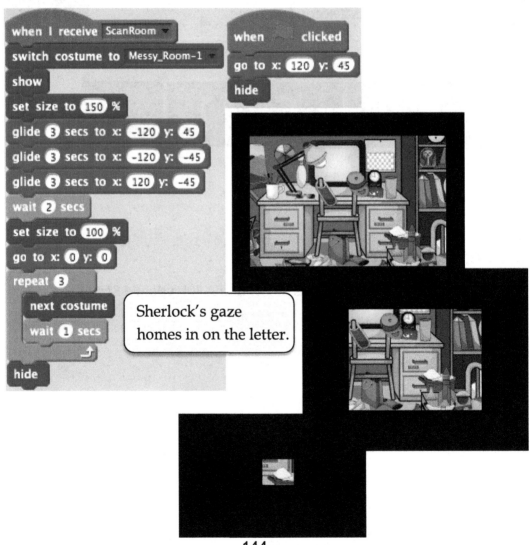

Sherlock's gaze homes in on the letter.

During the **NervousEyes** broadcast, Sherlock's face starts shaking. Go to the **Nervous Eyes** sprite.

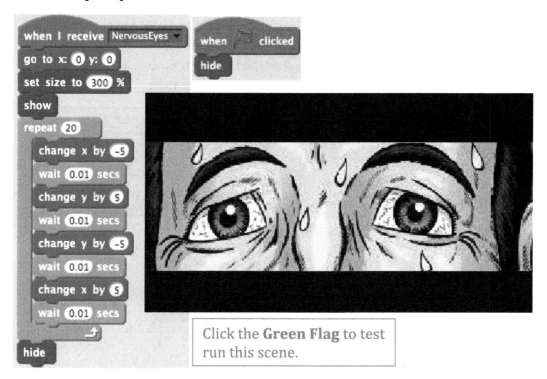

```
when I receive NervousEyes ▼
go to x: 0 y: 0
set size to 300 %
show
repeat 20
    change x by -5
    wait 0.01 secs
    change y by 5
    wait 0.01 secs
    change y by -5
    wait 0.01 secs
    change x by 5
    wait 0.01 secs
hide
```

```
when 🚩 clicked
hide
```

Click the **Green Flag** to test run this scene.

4. Program the Third Scene

Click the **Stage,** and drag the blocks below to the **Storyboard Script**.

```
switch backdrop to Black ▼
broadcast ReadDirections ▼ and wait
broadcast NewMission ▼ and wait
wait 1 secs
```

For the **ReadDirections** broadcast, go to the **Directions** sprite. This sprite slowly glides from the bottom to the top of the screen, which allows the audience to read what's inside.

```
when 🚩 clicked
set size to 200 %
go to x: 0 y: -450
hide
```

```
when I receive ReadDirections ▼
show
glide 15 secs to x: 0 y: 450
hide
```

145

Now let's do the **NewMission** broadcast. Go to the **TV** sprite.

Agent Smith appears on the TV and gives Sherlock the details of his mission. His mouth moves up and down during the sound recording.

Click the **Green Flag** to test run this scene.

5. Program the Fourth Scene

Click the **Stage** and drag the blocks below to the **Storyboard Script**.

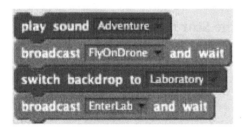

Now let's add additional code to the **Stage** for the **FlyOnDrone** broadcast message. In this broadcast, Sherlock flies on the drone while the background passes by in a blur.

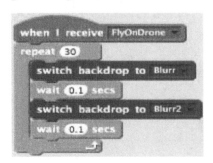

Now add the blocks below to the respective sprites.

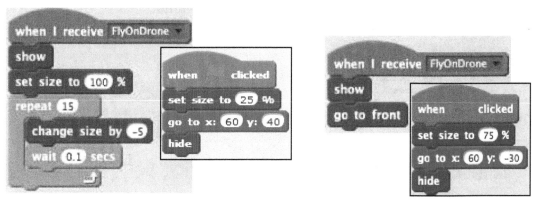

Sherlock   Drone

Next, let's program the **EnterLab** broadcast. Sherlock and his drone descend near one of the Laboratory's windows.

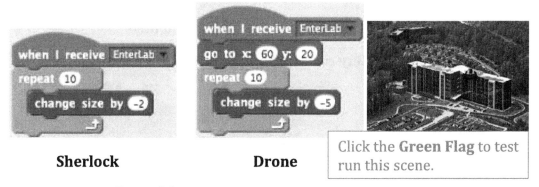

Sherlock   Drone   Click the **Green Flag** to test run this scene.

6. Program the Fifth Scene

Click the **Stage** and drag the blocks below to the **Storyboard Script**.

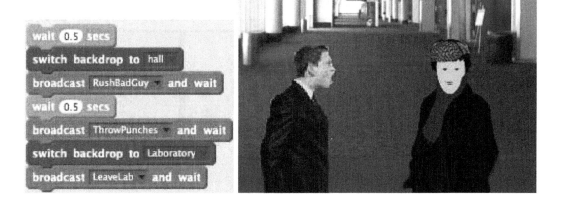

During the **RushBadGuy** broadcast, the **Bad Guy** appears, and **Sherlock** runs towards him. Meanwhile, the **drone** has been left behind.

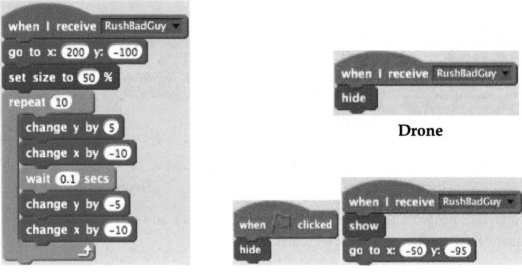

Sherlock

Drone

Bad Guy

When **Sherlock** and **Bad Guy** collide, **Sherlock** broadcasts **ThrowPunches** and defeats him.

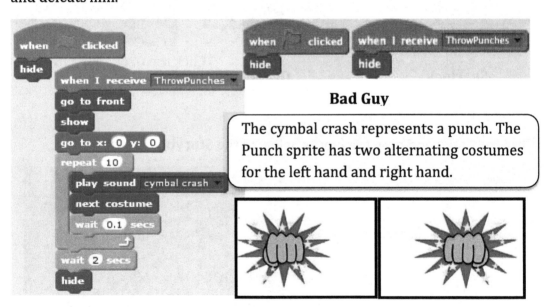

Bad Guy

The cymbal crash represents a punch. The Punch sprite has two alternating costumes for the left hand and right hand.

Punch

Now let's program the **LeaveLab** broadcast event. During this scene, **Sherlock** and his **Drone** exit the Laboratory from the window and fly away. **Sherlock** gives a parting wink.

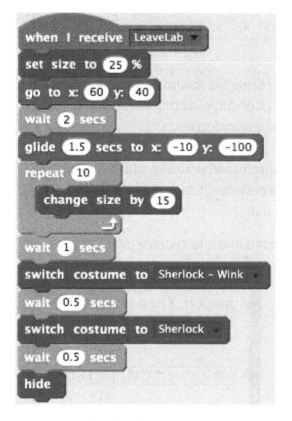

Sherlock

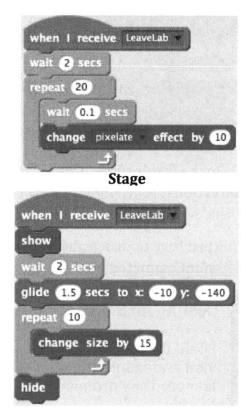

Stage

Drone

Click the **Green Flag** to test run this scene.

7. Program the Sixth Scene

Click the **Stage** and drag the blocks below to the **Storyboard Script**.

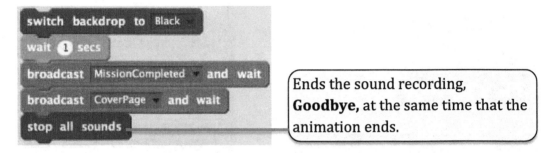

Ends the sound recording, **Goodbye,** at the same time that the animation ends.

Go to the **Letter** sprite. This sprite is programmed with the same code as the **Directions** sprite. Duplicate all of the **Direction** sprite's blocks. Drag-and-drop them over the **Letter** sprite in the sprite pane.

You just have to change the **When I Receive** block to receive the **MissionCompleted** broadcast.

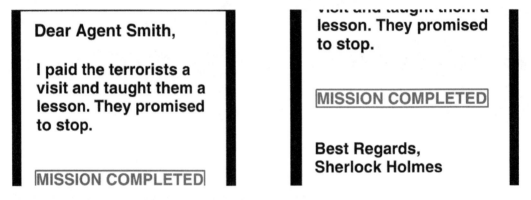

At the end of the animation, the **Shadow** sprite reappears on the screen during the broadcast, **CoverPage.** Add these last blocks to **Shadow:**

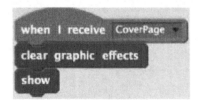

Now click the **Green Flag,** and enjoy your Sherlock Holmes animation!

150

CPSIA information can be obtained
at www.ICGtesting.com
Printed in the USA
LVOW05s0006240916
505972LV00010B/405/P